A Prayer Book

A Prayer Book

Robert A. Harris

.:Virtual**Salt**
Publishing
Tustin

A Prayer Book

VirtualSalt Publishing
Tustin, California
www.virtualsalt.com

ISBN 978-1-941233-19-1

Scripture quotations are from the translations indicated:
NASB New American Standard Bible
HCSB Holman Christian Standard Bible
NLT New Living Translation
GW God's Word
ERV Easy-to-read Version
CEV Contemporary English Version
ASV American Standard Version
ESV English Standard Version
NIV New International Version
KJV King James Version

All quotations from Brother Lawrence are from
the Donald Attwater translation.

22.22.22

Contents

Introduction

Then you will call upon Me and come and pray to Me, and I will listen to you.
— Jeremiah 29:12 (NASB)

"There are hundreds of books about prayer," you might be thinking. "How is this one different or better?" Some prayer books provide a collection of prayers, each of which is accompanied by a Scripture verse and sometimes a short devotional, while others offer commentary about prayer but include few examples. A number of them present Scripture passages as prayers.

This book, on the other hand, features a combination of practical discussions about what prayer is, what kinds there are, why and how to pray, together with many example prayers on a wide range of subjects that you can pray as they are written, customize to suit your own situation, or use as ideas to write your own prayers. In other words, the book is designed as a down-to-earth and up-to-heaven aid to help you improve your own prayers, both private and public, formal and informal.

But don't think the book contains stiff lectures about the theology of prayer, or a list of rigid rules and mandatory rituals. Instead, you will find the discussion filled with practical suggestions that will help you develop a better prayer life, and more importantly, a closer relationship with God. The formula is simple: (1) improving your prayer life, leads to (2) better communication with God, leads to (3) a closer relationship with God. Think of this book, then, as an interactive exercise in better communication—and hence a deeper love for our Lord.

Throughout the book are Scripture passages that provide the Biblical foundations for understanding prayer and its uses.

Discussion questions and activities for both individuals and groups have been added to enhance the book's use for individual and group study.

None of the ideas or suggestions in this book are meant to take the place of the work of the Holy Spirit in inspiring your prayers. Instead, the relationship between your mind, your heart, and the Spirit should only be enhanced by using the ideas here. Just as Jesus gave his disciples (and us) the Lord's prayer as a pattern to help us structure our heart thoughts, so too the examples and discussion here should give you the tools needed to help you connect better and find understanding through your prayers.

Thanks to my wife, Marie, and to Phil Robinette, David Mitchell, and Andre Mooney, who encouraged this project with good ideas.

Robert A. Harris
Tustin, California

1

What is Prayer?

Prayer is an invitation to God to intervene in our lives.
— Abraham Joshua Heschel

The simplest definition is that prayer is talking with God. That's straightforward enough, but the definition has several profound implications:

You're talking to your creator.

You are talking not only with the creator of your self, but with the creator of the universe, a creator who made everything, from the tiniest subatomic particles to the largest galaxies containing hundreds of trillions of stars (Genesis 1:16), each star with its own name (Isaiah 40:26); so remember always to be reverential and deferential. Prayer is an action of high seriousness, sometimes with dramatic consequences, even when thought or uttered while celebrating a wedding or watching a funny movie. And while skidding to a panic stop. Answered prayers change the universe every day.

✝
📖

The urgent request of a righteous person is very powerful in its effect.

—James 5:16 (HCSB)

This "high seriousness" doesn't mean that some subjects are too unimportant or that some requests are too small: By all means pray for the health of your dog, or to get a good parking space, or for your headache to go away; for with each of these "small" prayers you connect with God and draw a little closer to him. And, of course, give thanks for the food at every meal, however simple. Just remember in all prayers to show reverence and respect, remembering that God knows more than you do.

You're conversing with your best friend.

Because God is your friend, you can pray to him as you would talk with a friend. There is no need to fear entering his presence. Casual and informal and friendly—God is there whenever you need to praise him, thank him, or ask him for help. He's available as a best friend twenty-four hours a day.

✝
📖

You are My friends if you do what I command you.

—John 15:14 (NASB)

And because he is both your friend and your creator who knows you fully, you can express not only your love and gratitude, with deference and humility, but also your confusion, questions, doubts, fears, worries, frustrations, and failures, with boldness and freedom.

Whatever is on your mind, you can bring to God. Remember that God is not an aloof, distant being, nor is he an arrogant dictator before whom we must cower and tremble. Enter his presence with respect and humility and you will always be welcomed.

✝
📖

You will seek Me and find Me when you search for Me with all your heart.
                        —Jeremiah 29:13 (NASB)

You're building an intentional relationship.

Knowing and connecting with God begins with reading the Bible, where we learn about him, his directions for purposeful living, and his will for our lives. But God is more than a set of life rules or theological beliefs. God is a living being who desires relationship with his creatures. Praying to God enables us to develop our relationship with him. Once you begin to practice regular prayer to God, you will begin to connect with your creator in an intimate, personal way. Prayer shows that you are truly serious—intentional, purposeful, deliberate—about your friendship and God's sovereignty in your life.

If you say you believe in God, or even that you are a Christian, but you never pray to seek guidance, ask forgiveness, or thank the Giver, how exactly would you claim to have a relationship? What kind of relationship would you have with your spouse or best human friend if you hardly ever talked to each other?

The fact is, you cannot wish yourself closer to God. And you cannot have a deep relationship if you pray for ten seconds once a day before you start munching on your sandwich. To get to know God, and to grow in relationship, you must talk to him, share with him, seek his will, ask him, and worship him, every day. That's what prayer is all about.

God is waiting to hear from you.

✝

📖

Seek the LORD while He may be found;
Call upon Him while He is near.

—Isaiah 55:6 (NASB)

LOST INTIMACY

"Hello? Is this Marva?"

"Yes, this is Marva. Who's this?"

"It's Jake."

"Jake? Jake who?"

"Jake Perry. Remember me?"

"Oh, yes. From college. Hi, Jake Perry. How are you?"

"Fine, fine. In fact, I've been thinking about you for a long time."

"Oh? Why?"

"You see, I've always thought highly of you ever since we first met in music class."

"Music class? That was—."

"And I finally decided to ask you out so we could, you know, get acquainted and develop a relationship."

"Jake, music class was, what, six, seven years ago?"

"I know. And I've been thinking about developing a relationship with you ever since. I've even started to pray about it."

"Well, I'm certainly flattered, but I'm sorry, Jake. You're too late."

"But why? What do you mean?"

"If you wanted a relationship with me, you should have said something way back when. Right now, I've been married for four years and have two kids."

There's a crucial difference—a gulf—between *believing in God* and *believing God*; and between *knowing about God* and *knowing God*. Prayer provides that bridge.

✝
📖

I will give them a heart to know Me, for I am the LORD; and they will be My people, and I will be their God, for they will return to Me with their whole heart.

—Jeremiah 24:7 (NASB)

By developing a relationship with God through prayer and worship, we can become his children:

✝
📖

"And I will be a father to you,
And you shall be sons and daughters to Me,"
Says the Lord Almighty.

—2 Corinthians 6:18 (NASB)

You can speak in ordinary language.

Since you are talking with your best friend, it follows that you can talk the same way you do with any friend. You don't need to use those old kinds of address, such as the informal pronouns *thou, thee, thy* and

so forth. Nor do you need an artificially exalted language, a dramatic tone of voice, clichés, or "poetic"
word order. You need not pray like this:

℘ 🕊 ℘
A FLOWERY PRAYER

Oh thou greatest God of gods, thou master of each
one of us, thine unworthy creatures, we thee beseech
upon thy vile children to condescend and render un-
to us thy grace that surpasseth all understanding. . . .

However, if creating that kind of prayer makes you
feel comfortable and closer to God, it's all right. The
situation is similar to that of Bible readers who prefer
the King James translation. A friend once told me, "If
I'm reading some modern translation instead of the
King James, I don't feel like I'm reading God's word."
So, if a certain prayer style makes you feel nearer to
God, and if that feeling reflects a genuine drawing
nearer to God, it's perfectly all right. But if this overly
formal style keeps you mentally or emotionally at a
distance from God, you should reconsider.

Before you fix on a style for communicating, try
this example, as a pattern for seeking God's will in a
job search, election, operation, or other event:

℘ 🕊 ℘
A PRAYER FOR GOD'S WILL

Dear Lord, creator of every good thing, from the
universe to our own souls, we ask for your help and
sovereignty in the outcome of this [event]. Do your
will in the outcome, and if it might please you, we
ask that the [event] will be successful. We thank you
in Jesus' name. Amen.

And now try this, quite informal, style, with the same subject:

A PRAYER FOR PEACE OF HEART

Dear Lord, I know you know what's best for me, and I pray for your will in how this all turns out. But I come to you in my anxiety, seeking your peace. I put this [event] into your hands and pray that you will take control. If it pleases you, may this [event] be successful. Please relieve my stress as you do your will. I thank you and I praise you. In Jesus' name. Amen.

Choose the style you want, then. Just remember that if you use an artificial style when praying aloud in a group, your prayers may come across as less sincere, or in the worst case, fake. The assumption is that when your heart is truly in a prayer, you don't have time for fancifying it or "arting it up." People know that serious communication, as when you talk to your boss, uses clear and direct language. It's best, then, to avoid the unnaturally ornate style, so that people aren't tempted to think your prayers are artificial, meaning insincere, meaning fake.

You're involving your whole being.
All prayers—even those that ask for something—are a form of worship because they recognize that God is our Lord and sustainer. Our prayers reflect not just our dependence on God but our love for him. And love includes our entire being. When asked what was the most important commandment, Jesus answered that it was to love God. But notice how he amplified it:

✝
📖

You shall love the Lord your God with all your
heart, and with all your soul, and with all your
mind, and with all your strength.
— Mark 12:30 (NASB)

Therefore, when we express our love to God through
prayer, we must include our whole self. We must pray
from the heart (our feelings or emotions); we must
pray with our soul (our living being or life), we must
pray with our minds (our thinking, our intellect), and
we must pray with our strength (our energy, our power). Pray from the depths of who you are, combining
thought and feeling, life and strength.

You should listen as well as speak.

Remember that, because prayer is a conversation
with God, you shouldn't do all the talking. You should
not talk *at* God, the way some people talk at their
friends by blabbing in unending sentences. Pause, and
pause often and for a good period of time, and listen.
The Holy Spirit is often soft spoken.

✝
📖

Meditate in your heart upon your bed, and be still.
— Psalm 4:4b (NASB)

In fact, when you are ready to pray, before you
start talking, why not "establish yourself in the presence of God" (to paraphrase Brother Lawrence), and
listen quietly for a while? [1]

---

[1] See Chapter 7 about establishing yourself in the presence of God.

ℬ 🕊 ℛ

A PRAYER FOR ATTENTIVENESS TO GOD

Lord, I come into your holy and loving presence just to be with you and to listen to you. May I hear you when your Spirit whispers and when we meet heart to heart. In Jesus' name. Amen.

†
📖

Be still, and know that I am God.
— Psalm 46:10a (KJV)

George Herbert's definition of prayer.

We close this discussion about the definition of prayer by looking at a thought-provoking sonnet by seventeenth century English poet George Herbert. Herbert describes prayer in a series of phrases that seem to reveal a struggle to find a suitable analogy. The result is a collection of images that reveal the complexity and the richness of prayer, with its various purposes and effects.

PRAYER

Prayer, the Church's banquet, Angel's age,
God's breath in man returning to his birth,
The soul in paraphrase, heart in pilgrimage,
The Christian plummet sounding heav'n and earth;
Engine against the Almighty, sinners' tower,
Reverséd thunder, Christ-side-piercing spear,
The six-days' world transposing in an hour,
A kind of tune, which all things hear and fear;
Softness, and peace, and joy, and love, and bliss,
Exalted Manna, gladness of the best,
Heaven in ordinary, man well dressed,
The Milky Way, the bird of Paradise,
Church-bells beyond the stars heard, the soul's blood,

The land of spices; something understood.

As you can see, near the end of the poem, the poet, after trying several ever-more dramatic images, suddenly stops searching for an adequate comparison and concludes with the key idea that ultimately, prayer is "something understood."

Note, in passing, the dramatic and thought-provoking power of figurative language. So many of the images here cause our minds to take flight and think more deeply ("the soul in paraphrase," "Christ side-piercing spear," "the soul's blood"). Images, especially vivid images, merge thought and feeling and imagination to create a dynamic impact. (See Chapter 16 for a discussion of figurative language in prayer. And see the end of this chapter for some explanations of Herbert's poem.)

✠✠✠

Chapter 1 Questions for Thought and Discussion
1. After reading this chapter, has your idea about the nature of prayer changed? Explain.
2. How would you define prayer?
3. How do you reconcile talking to God as your friend and as your creator?
4. How can you love God with "all your soul" and "all your strength"?

Chapter 1 Activity: Definitions of Prayer
Consult dictionaries, encyclopedias, books of prayer, the Internet, friends, and family, collecting many different definitions of prayer.
1. What do these definitions have in common?

2. How do the definitions differ?
3. What is the significance of the commonalities?
4. What is the significance of the differences?
5. Has the range of definitions given you insight or understanding into prayer? Explain.

Chapter 1 Group Activities

1. Have each member of the group write out a definition of prayer. Share definitions and together use them to construct a single, best definition. What was added? What was changed? What makes this definition better than any of the single ones? If there is disagreement, what is the sticking point?

2. Have the members of the group join into groups of two or three. One member is to describe to another member a prayer request or a prayer topic of interest. The other member is to write a short prayer covering that request or topic. The prayer must be written from the perspective of the first member (the requester). So, for example, instead of writing a prayer for Bill that says, "Lord, please help Bill pass the entrance exam," the text would say, "Lord, please help me pass the entrance exam." Discuss the results first between requester and writer, then in the small group.

Suggested explications of George Herbert's "Prayer"

the Church's banquet. A church full of praying people can send a banquet full (a buffet) of varied prayers to God.

Angel's age. Prayer has existed from the time of the creation of the angels, which is the beginning of time.

God's breath. God breathed life into man, and now man is returning breath to God through prayer.

The soul in paraphrase. One's life principle restated.

Heart in pilgrimage. The heart humbly travels toward God.

The Christian plummet. A weighted string that measures the depth of both heaven and earth.

Engine against the Almighty. A machine that "attacks" God to break down the obstacles to communication.

Sinners' tower. A tower built to attack forts, this one built by sinners. Prayer is thus a siege engine. The tower also suggests a place of refuge and safety.

Reverséd thunder. Prayer sends thunder back to God, as a loud message from humans.

Christ-side-piercing spear. Prayer enters deeply into the Lord's being, like the spear that pierced his side at the crucifixion.

The six-days' world . . . An answered prayer can quickly affect the entire creation that God made in six days.

A kind of tune. . . Prayer penetrates the heart and soul, like music.

Softness. . . Prayer produces emotions similar to the feelings generated by these things.

Exalted Manna. The original manna came down from heaven. Prayer is like manna going up to heaven.

Gladness of the best. The way we feel glad at finding the best example or best quality in something.

Heaven in ordinary, man well dressed. Prayer is the ordinary ornament of heaven, and the tuxedo of humans.

The Milky Way, the bird of Paradise. Prayer is compared to the massive and the beautiful, both awe inspiring.

Church-bells beyond the stars heard. God hears us from heaven.

The soul's blood. Prayer is the life-giving principle of our souls.

The land of spices. The sweet aroma of spices. Remember that incense was burned to worship God. And compare Psalm 141:2.

Something understood. Prayer is understanding, God and oneself.

2

What Are the Ways to Pray?

Prayer is practicing the presence of God.
— Brother Lawrence[2]

Rather than defining prayer as talking with God, perhaps we should take George Herbert's idea from his sonnet quoted in Chapter 1, that prayer is "something understood" between us and God. So, a better definition of prayer might be "communicating with God," because there are several ways to pray — or to be intentionally in God's presence — in addition to talking. Here are some of the ways.

Pray the words of your heart.

Even though you might be new to talking with God, and even though you at first might feel tongue-tied and inarticulate, just relax and say what's on your heart. Recall from Chapter 1 that you are in the pres-

---

[2] The *Practice of the Presence of God* was compiled from the conversations and letters of Brother Lawrence in the late seventeenth century. I highly recommend the book. Several editions and translations are available.

ence of a good friend, who is eager to hear what you have to say.

Begin by thanking God for some blessing, whether a specific one, such as meeting a new friend or getting paid or enjoying a meal; or whether it is general gratitude for life and health, a place to live, or your salvation.

If you start to think about your blessings, you'll have plenty to say. For example,

ෆ 🕊 ෨
A PRAYER GIVING THANKS

Dear Lord, thank you so much for all the blessings that you so generously heap upon us. We are so grateful for a clean water supply, dependable cars, a reliable phone system, plenty of food, and the blessing of friends and loved ones. Thank you for watching over us and guiding us in the path you have appointed for us. . . .

Once again: If you can think of nothing else, and if you feel uncomfortable at first asking for God's help with something, then you can always begin by expressing your gratitude. The more you think about how blessed your life is — in spite of the problems you might have — the more grateful and the happier you will be.

ෆ 🕊 ෨
A PRAYER OF GRATITUDE

Lord, thank you for being available to me twenty-four hours a day, to listen when I need you and need your help. I'm always in need of something, and I'm so grateful that you're near when I seek your help. Even when you answer in a way I don't understand, I appreciate your love and care. Thank you for being the God of the universe, and for being my God and Father, too. . . .

Write a letter to God.

If you are a letter writer or someone who likes to journal, but you don't feel comfortable praying without some forethought, consider writing a letter to God, and include your thankfulness, your praise, and your requests. When you are satisfied with your final draft, read the letter as a prayer.

ଛ 🕊 ଔ

A PRAYER FOR HELP WITH STRESS

Dear Lord, you know how totally stressed out I am over [this issue]. Please take this burden from me onto your strong shoulders and give me peace and rest. Refresh my mind and heart as I turn this issue over to you. Let me rely on you to carry me through the tension and to trust in you for the outcome. Thank you for being my strength when I am weak and for bringing me calm when I am stressed. In Jesus' name. Amen.

Read the Bible back to God.

The Bible contains many prayers that you can read aloud or silently and make them your prayers.

A favorite example is Psalm 23, here as it was translated by the poet George Herbert in the seventeenth century:

ଛ 🕊 ଔ

PSALM 23

The God of love my shepherd is,

And he that doth me feed:
While he is mine, and I am his,
What can I want or need?

He leads me to the tender grass,
Where I both feed and rest;
Then to the streams that gently pass:
In both I have the best.

Or if I stray, he doth convert
And bring my mind in frame:
And all this not for my desert,
But for his holy name.

Yea, in death's shady black abode
Well may I walk, not fear:
For thou art with me: and thy rod
To guide, thy staff to bear.

Nay, thou dost make me sit and dine,
Even in my enemy's sight:
My head with oil, my cup with wine
Runs over day and night.

Surely thy sweet and wondrous love
Shall measure all my days;
And as it never shall remove,
So neither shall my praise.

Many of the Psalms can be prayed directly, as with
Psalm 8, here from the NASB:

✝
📖
PSALM 8

O LORD, our Lord,
How majestic is Your name in all the earth,

Who have displayed Your splendor above the heavens!
From the mouth of infants and nursing babes You have
established strength
Because of Your adversaries,
To make the enemy and the revengeful cease.
When I consider Your heavens, the work of Your fingers,
The moon and the stars, which You have ordained,
What is man that You take thought of him,
And the son of man that You care for him?
Yet You have made him a little lower than God,
And You crown him with glory and majesty!
You make him to rule over the works of Your hands;
You have put all things under his feet,
All sheep and oxen,
And also the beasts of the field,
The birds of the heavens and the fish of the sea,
Whatever passes through the paths of the seas.
O LORD, our Lord,
How majestic is Your name in all the earth!
— Psalm 8 (NASB)

When you want to pray Biblical passages, you might want to use one of the more informal translations that render Scripture into an everyday language, so that it is easier to feel the prayer. Here, for example, is Psalm 8 in the Contemporary English Version:

†
📖
PSALM 8

Our LORD and Ruler, your name is wonderful everywhere on earth! You let your glory be seen in the heavens above. With praises from children and from tiny infants, you have built a fortress. It makes your enemies silent, and all who turn against you are left speechless. I often think of the heavens your hands have made, and of the moon and stars you put in place. Then I ask, "Why do you care about us humans? Why are you concerned for us weaklings?" You made us a little lower than you yourself, and you have crowned us with glory and honor. You let us rule everything your hands have made. And you put all of it under our power—the sheep and the cattle, and every wild animal, the birds in the sky, the fish in the sea, and all ocean creatures. Our LORD and Ruler, your name is wonderful every-where on earth!

— Psalm 8 (CEV)

Other informal translations include the *Easy-to-Read Version* (ERV), the *Good News Bible* (GNB), *God's Word* (GW) and the *New Living Translation* (NLT).

Much of the Bible discusses God's goodness and guidance in the third person ("God is good"). If you want, you can refocus the Scripture passages so that they are prayers addressing God directly ("God, you are good.") For example, Psalm 19:1 reads:

✝
📖

The heavens are telling of the glory of God;
And their expanse is declaring the work of His hands.

— Psalm 19:1 (NASB)

You could pray it directly to God this way:

ဢ 🕊 ര
PSALM 19:1

The heavens are telling of Your glory O God;
And their expanse is declaring the work of Your hands.

Read a prewritten prayer.

In addition to this book, there are hundreds, if not thousands, of books with prayers in them that you can pray. Read the prayer first, to see whether it fits your needs and embodies your intentions. Then read the prayer intentionally as a prayer. Read it aloud or silently. God can hear you either way.

Here is an example prayer for decision making:

ॐ 🕊 ॐ
A PRAYER FOR DECISION MAKING

Dear Lord, this is a big decision and I want you to help me with it. Please send your Holy Spirit to illuminate my mind and give me wisdom in the choice. Don't let my ego or selfish desires get in the way. If you have a specific choice for me, let me know what it is. Thank you for your love, care, and goodness. In Jesus' name, Amen.

Read a poem.

Many poems address God and can be converted into prayers simply by praying them. Some of the most beautiful Christian poems come from 16th and 17th century poets such as George Herbert, Anne Bradstreet, Philip Sidney, Edward Taylor, and John Donne. Other poems discuss love, the natural world, hopes and fears, or other subjects that might at the time be close to your heart. You can read these to God as your contribution to your time of sharing with the Lord.

Remember that the words to hymns are poems that can be read and prayed. For example, God can be praised by reading the words from "This Is My Father's World," by Maltbie D. Babcock:

ဆာ 🕊 ୟ
A POEM PRAYER

This is my Father's world, and to my listening ears
All nature sings, and round me rings the music of
the spheres.
This is my Father's world: I rest me in the thought
Of rocks and trees, of skies and seas;
His hand the wonders wrought.

This is my Father's world, the birds their carols raise,
The morning light, the lily white, declare their Mak-
er's praise.
This is my Father's world: He shines in all that's fair;
In the rustling grass I hear Him pass;
He speaks to me everywhere.

This is my Father's world. O let me ne'er forget
That though the wrong seems oft so strong, God is
the ruler yet.
This is my Father's world: the battle is not done:
Jesus Who died shall be satisfied,
And earth and Heav'n be one.

Read from a devotional.

Many devotionals include prayers, but even those
that do not can be useful during your prayer time. As
with the poems mentioned above, you can read the devotional entry to God and commune with him through
the Spirit.

Recite a prayer couplet.

A good way to teach children to pray is to let them
memorize couplets (in addition to Scripture). A couplet
is a two-line rhyming poem. However, there is no rule

that adults cannot memorize or even write and then memorize such couplets.

Here is a sampling:

ॐ 🕊 ☙
EXAMPLE COUPLET POEM-PRAYERS

Dear Lord, please help me serve you in this day,
And guide in all I do and think and say.

Forgive, O God, the sin that I have done,
And mercy grant through Jesus Christ your Son.

In this, dear Lord, please help me choose the right,
For you are my one true and guiding light.

Inspire, O Lord, the words I now must speak;
May they produce the outcome that I seek.

We thank you, Lord, for all this food today,
And pray you'll bless it to us every way.

Say a prayer from childhood.

Your parents might have taught you one or more prayers to memorize as a child. If you recall these, pray them to the Lord.

ॐ 🕊 ☙
EXAMPLE CHILDHOOD PRAYER

Now I lay me down to sleep.
I pray the Lord my soul to keep.
If I should die before I wake,
I pray the Lord my soul to take.
If I should live for further days,

I pray the Lord to guide my ways.

Note here that one of the great benefits of having God as our creator and sustainer is that no sincere praise and worship to him will be rejected or laughed at. We can say a child's prayer, sing off key, or use bad grammar, and God will still accept our prayers.

Sing a worship song or hymn.

Singing is a great way to commune with God because the music of a song reaches directly into your emotions while the words reach your mind. And you can sing along with a recording of a song, intending it as a prayer. The musicians will stand by you, so to speak, if you are too shy to sing acapella. The musical accompaniment can encourage you even if you have an off-key voice.

A wide variety of song music is available. For example, there are many worship choruses with some impacting words and music.

Remember any of these?

I love you Lord, and I lift my voice, to worship you. . . .

Lord, you are more precious than silver. . . .

Wonderful, merciful savior, precious redeemer and friend. . . .

Ancient words, ever true, changing me and changing you. . . .

And there are classic hymns such as "Take My Life and Let It Be," "And Can It Be that I Should Gain," and "Amazing Grace." Even if you absolutely dare not sing aloud, you can still listen to the songs as a prayer to God, intending the praise for him.

✝
📖
Sing to God, O kingdoms of the earth,
Sing praises to the Lord.
— Psalm 68:32 (NASB)

Groan with the Spirit.

In times of great grief or stress or uncertainty or pain, we sometimes simply cannot put into words what we are feeling. But that doesn't mean we can't communicate with our best friend. One reason God has put his Holy Spirit into us when we are saved is to help us connect—and stay connected—to him. And this is especially true in times of distress:

✝
📖
In the same way the Spirit also helps our weakness; for we do not know how to pray as we should, but the Spirit Himself intercedes for us with groanings too deep for words.
— Romans 8:26 (NASB)

Usually prayer is a question of groaning rather than speaking, tears rather than words.
— Augustine

Listen.

Ever meet someone whose idea of a conversation is to talk your ears off? Someone who talks at you rather than with you? Someone who speaks in two-thousand-word sentences, with no commas? Don't be like that with God. Certainly, he is eager to hear all your problems and frustrations, but, as I said in Chapter 1, conversation should be a two-way street, where people exchange ideas and experiences, hopes and fears, offers and requests. And that is what prayer should be.

Listening is important, and should be done quietly, for the Lord through his Spirit often speaks softly and without drama:

†
📖

Then He said, "Go out and stand on the mountain in the LORD's presence." At that moment, the LORD passed by. A great and mighty wind was tearing at the mountains and was shattering cliffs before the LORD, but the LORD was not in the wind. After the wind there was an earthquake, but the LORD was not in the earthquake. After the earthquake there was a fire, but the LORD was not in the fire. And after the fire there was a voice, a soft whisper.
—1 Kings 19:11-12 (HCSB)

†
📖

If only My people would listen to Me!
—Psalm 81:13a (HCSB)

If you're unsure about how to listen, find a quiet location and open the Bible to the Psalms, or to any book of the Scriptures. Before you read, pray that the

Holy Spirit will give you understanding of the Word and insight into God's truth.

℘ 🕊 ℥

A PRAYER BEFORE READING THE BIBLE

Dear Lord, please send your Holy Spirit to enlighten my understanding as I read your word in the Bible. Teach me your perfect truth as I read, and let me know any specific message you have for me. Speak to me through your word. I thank you in Jesus' name. Amen.

After reading, pray about what you have read, and include one or more of these elements into your thoughts:

- Summarize or explain what the passage said. Describe the situation, the event, the context.
- Explain what the passage means. Clarify the message, identify and explain the figurative language.
- Describe the effect the passage had on those who heard the speech or witnessed the events
- Apply the meaning of the passage to your own life. How does the Scripture give you knowledge of God, instructions for behavior, or insight into human nature?

We are so used to the busy environment around us that we often forget to stop and listen for the Lord.

✝
📖

Be still, and know that I am God. I will be exalted among the nations, I will be exalted in the earth!
—Psalm 46:10 (ESV)

Summary.

So, what are the ways to pray? Or how should you pray? Every way and always. God accepts every mode of communication, just as he speaks every language. So a prayer can be any communication you have with God: Your own words, aloud or quietly, words read or recited or sung to God, or just an emotional feeling of joy or gratitude—or even grief—directed to him.

✠✠✠

Chapter 2 Questions for Thought and Discussion
1. How many of the ways to pray have you used? Which do you prefer and why?
2. Has reading this chapter caused you to pray in a way you did not previously use? What has been the result?
3. If you have children, do you plan to (or do you now) write prayers for them to say or memorize?

Chapter 2 Activities
1. Write down a childhood prayer and pray it.
2. Compose a prayer suitable for young children to memorize and pray.

Chapter 2 Group Activity
1. Have each group member share a favorite or unusual way to pray, whether one of those listed in the chapter or a new one. Each member should explain why it is effective or useful.

3

Why Should We Pray?

To contact God, the username is your name and the pass-word is PRAYER.
— Anonymous

In part, because we are steeped in a culture of narcissism and self-indulgence, we usually think of prayer as asking God for something — healing, guidance, help on a test or getting a job. All these, of course, are good reasons to pray. We depend on God's help and guidance in order to live the best lives. But there are many other circumstances, many other topics, many other reasons that can bring us to prayer. Here are a few of the answers to the question, Why should we pray? As you read these, see if you can add to the list.

To show gratitude.

To my mind, nearly every prayer should begin with thanksgiving to God for his lavish and undeserved blessings that he has heaped upon us. It's one thing to be an ungrateful society where every gift is seen as an entitlement. But to think of the grace and mercy of God that way is unconscionable.

ℰ 🕊 ℛ

A PRAYER TO SHOW GRATITUDE

Dear Lord, thank you so much for blessing me with the beginning of a new day. I bless your name for your goodness and kindness to me. Thank you for saving me from a lost life and bringing me into your kingdom. Your gifts to me are unending, and I am grateful all the more as I remember that I don't deserve any of them. I deeply appreciate you, Lord. Thank you for Jesus. Amen.

ℰ 🕊 ℛ

A PRAYER OF THANKSGIVING FOR FOOD

Thanks so much, dear Lord, for all these tasty and nourishing groceries you have blessed us with. We are so blessed to be able to afford all this quality and variety in our food. I pray that you will bless it to the nourishment and strengthening of our bodies when we eat it, and that we will serve you with the energy it gives us. We thank you again in humble gratitude for your love, care, and generosity. In Jesus' name. Amen.

Prayer is an excellent way to show your gratitude to God for every blessing. For example, why not pause a moment to give thanks even if you're just getting a snack?

True confession: I say a brief prayer of thanks every time I take a drink of ice water, because it's my favorite beverage and it tastes so clean and delicious. To me, it's one of God's most brilliant creations.

ఐ 🕊 ౪
A PRAYER OF THANKSGIVING FOR GRAPES

Thank you very much, our dear Lord, for making available to us these fresh and delicious table grapes. Bless all the hands that grew, harvested, and brought them to us so that we could enjoy a summer fruit at any time and in any season. And thank you for giving us the money to afford them. In Jesus' name. Amen.

✝
📖

O give thanks to the LORD, for He is good;
For His lovingkindness is everlasting.
—1 Chronicles 16:34 (NASB)

INGRATITUDE

"Hey, there, Sallie. Did I just see you throw a dinner plate up against the block wall?"

"Maybe. What's it to you, Deb?"

"Whatever made you do that?"

"I'm mad at God."

"So you're breaking dishes? Wh—."

"Did you hear that Edith Mae married that guy with a gillion dollars?"

"No, but who cares?"

"I care because God's given me nothin', and I'm mad at him. Edith Mae rides in a stretch limo, eats fancy food, has a rich and handsome husband who buys her expensive jewelry and takes her on round the world vacations. And I got nothin'."

"I don't know about that, Sal. Look, you've got a good husband who puts up with you, four bratty kids to love, a dry house to live in, a cute dog, a dependable car, a good job—."

"Job? See, Deb? I have to work all day to keep from starving, while Edith Mae probably sits at home watching TV and eating chocolate bonbons all day."

"So you're mad at God because he hasn't arranged your life in a way that lets you grow brain dead from binge watching the idiot box while stuffing your face with bonbons until you're too fat to fit through the door."

"Well, not only that—."

"Sallie, you have the blessings of food, shelter, love, and health—oh, and enough spare time to complain that you don't have a collection of sparkly ornaments to hang on your body. Yes, I can see why you'd be mad at God."

"Huh? Well, then, you understand."

"Oh, yeah, right. What I don't understand is why lightning doesn't strike someone near here."

"What are you talking about? Did you say lightning? Is a storm coming? I don't see any clouds."

To praise God.

Accompanying the heartfelt appreciation for God's goodness should be words of praise for the creator of all things beautiful.

ഔ 🕊 ൪

A PRAYER TO PRAISE GOD

Lord, I praise you and honor you for all your goodness. I praise you for the beauty and wonders of your creation. How exalted you are as the maker of the universe, from the smallest grain of sand to the largest galaxy. And blessed be your name in every circumstance, giving us wonderful gifts from your infinite store of blessings, and even making harms and hurts work for ultimate good for those who love you. May your name be forever exalted. In Jesus' name. Amen.

✝

📖

Praise the LORD! Praise, O servants of the LORD, Praise the name of the LORD.

—Psalm 113:1 (NASB)

ഓ 🕊 രു

A PRAYER TO SHOW GRATITUDE AND PRAISE

Thank you so much, dear Lord, for answering my prayer and bringing me success in my [endeavor]. I rejoice in your grace and praise you and bless you and thank you again and again. I know I don't deserve your goodness, and that's one reason I thank you all the more. I really appreciate your help with my [endeavor]. Without your gracious blessing, I'd still be trying to succeed. With gratefulness, dear Lord, I pray in Jesus' name. Amen.[3]

To worship God.

Worshipping God means to offer him respect, honor, and reverence. We worship God by exalting him and by humbling ourselves before him. By quietly worshipping God, we affirm our sense of his holiness, worthiness, and goodness. We not only acknowledge God's authority, but we joyfully exalt him as worthy to have authority over us.

ഓ 🕊 രു

A PRAYER TO WORSHIP GOD

My dear Lord, I bow down before you in worship and adoration. I exalt you for being who you are— holy and good and perfect. With utmost reverence I

---

[3] I was prompted to write this prayer of thankfulness after the Lord answered my prayer about fixing a window.

pray that you will continue to be ever blessed as you are ever a blessing to me. And as Jesus taught us to say in the Lord's prayer, may your name be hallowed and honored forever throughout the earth. In the name of Jesus. Amen.

To draw closer to God.

Even though God is always with us, and his Holy Spirit is within us, we sometimes feel distant from God and want to draw closer to him again. Prayer is an excellent way to do this because while in prayer, we are spending time with God. In *The Practice of the Presence of God*, Brother Lawrence reminds us that relationships grow closer through time spent together:

> We must know before we can love; and to know God we must often think about Him. And when we love Him, we shall think about Him all the more, "for where thy treasure is, there is thy heart also."
> — Ninth Letter

If we want to grow closer to God, we must learn more about him and from him. Making a deliberate effort to enter his presence by prayer and by reading his word will bring us nearer. Brother Lawrence again:

> We must concentrate on knowing God: The more we know Him, the more we want to know Him. And, as knowledge is commonly the measure of love, the deeper and wider our knowledge, the greater will be our love.
> — Sixteenth Letter

જી 🕊 ભ

A PRAYER TO DRAW CLOSER TO GOD

Dear God, please help me to come closer to you and to stay with you. Don't let my busyness interfere with our time together, but instead help me make you the priority of my day and my life. Give me the wisdom to seek your heart in all that I do. Draw me to you when I am too weak or preoccupied to make the first move. May you be ever blessed and ever my true friend. I thank you and praise you. In Jesus' name. Amen.

✝
📖

Draw near to God and He will draw near to you.
—James 4:8a (NASB)

To seek guidance.

There are at least two kinds of prayer for guidance. First is the prayer suitable for daily use, that asks God to be our guide in the course of our lives.

જી 🕊 ભ

A PRAYER FOR GOD'S GUIDANCE

Dear God, please guide and direct my life today, being sovereign in all that I do, say, and think. Show me the way to proceed in my activities and point out the right choice in each decision. Thank you for your goodness to me and for your help. In Jesus' name. Amen.

Second is the prayer for guidance through a specific situation. Sometimes we don't know what to do or which way to go. We can't make a decision because we haven't even identified the choices available. Or we have what appears to be all bad alternatives. When we get to the end of the rope, we think two things: First, we recognize the need for God's guidance, and second, we wonder why we waited so long to pray for it.

As you pray this prayer, understand that God is both caring and mighty to save.

ഇ 🕊 ര
A PRAYER FOR GOD'S SPECIFIC GUIDANCE

Dear Lord, I must admit that I don't know what to do now. I feel stuck, with no good options. What should I do? I really need your help and direction. Please guide me into a path that will honor and please you, a path that will also move me forward and not backward. Please keep me from giving in to an easy but wrong choice, and deliver me from those who would offer me moral shortcuts. Be my North Star, and let me navigate through this by your light. I thank you and praise you. In Jesus' name. Amen.

To affirm in God's presence what you care about.

It is said that you can learn almost all you need to know about a person by looking at his or her credit and debit card statements. For what you spend your money on tells us what you truly value, what your priorities are, even who you are.

Similarly, you can understand what is important to you just by noting what you pray about. Are you always praying for yourself, or for more stuff? Or do you pray for others and for God's will in your life and in the world?

Once we understand that the things we pray for represent the most important things to us, we can understand why we pray. After all, if God already knows what we need and want and hope and plan, then why pray? It's not as if we are telling him something new.

God isn't sitting up in heaven listening to us pray and thinking, "Oh, you have the flu? And you want me to speed up your recovery? Why didn't you say so sooner? I mean, who knew?" Instead, he wants to know what we think about having the flu. Do we want his help? Do we still trust him? Will we draw closer to him through this? Or are we going to whine and complain and blame?

A main reason we pray, then, is to enable us to sort out our priorities in the presence of God and to remind ourselves that we are dependent on him for everything. Prayer clarifies our thoughts. Essayist Francis Bacon says that in the company of a friend, a speaker

> tosses his thoughts more easily; he marshals them more orderly; he sees how they look when they are turned into words. . . .
>
> — Of Friendship

So, when we pray to our friend the Lord, we discover what we really think when our thoughts "are turned into words," in this case, prayers.

ℬℒℛ

A PRAYER FOR GOD'S HELP

Dear Lord, you know my many needs, and the needs of my loved ones. Please be gracious to us and guide us in our daily lives, protect us from harm, and deliver us from sin and evil. I pray today especially for [my issue]. Please help me resolve it according to your will. I thank you and praise you, in Jesus' name. Amen.

ಕಾ 🕊 ಞ

A PRAYER FOR PRIORITIES

Dear Lord, I'm confused and conflicted by too many demands, too many tasks, and too many choices. Everything seems to be Priority One, and yet much of the time I feel as if I'm wasting time and effort. Please help me, O Lord, to organize my days around the tasks that are the most important, and the tasks you want me to put first. Guide me through your Holy Spirit to make better choices and to spend my time here on earth in a way that pleases you and serves you. Thank you so very much. In Jesus' name I pray. Amen.

In a word, God wants us to know our own hearts, what we truly value, what things we place above other things. What do we really want, as opposed to what we tell others—or even ourselves—what we really want? The answer to that may come only when we are talking to our maker and heavenly Father, to whom we dare not pretend or dissemble.

To resist temptation.

In Biblical times, temptation was raw and ever present. In those days the shortcutters were everywhere, trying either to con others or to convince others to join them in taking the "easy way."

✝
📖

Keep watching and praying that you may not come into temptation; the spirit is willing, but the flesh is weak.

—Mark 14:38 (NASB)

In addition to those common temptations arising from greed and lust, today the world is filled with temptations that our ancestors never experienced. For example, much of the business of marketing is to promote products through temptation. In other words, we are not only subject to the temptations that naturally arise in our sinful hearts, but we are confronted by temptations manufactured for us by the marketing folks.

Remember the traditional Seven Deadly Sins? Pride, Greed (or Avarice), Anger (or Wrath), Gluttony, Lust, Envy, and Sloth. Now think of them as temptations to sin—in other words, as advertisements:

Pride. "We do it all for you." "You deserve this." "You're number one." "This is for a select few like you." "This isn't for just anyone." "You're special." "This isn't for ordinary people. It's for you." "Live your uniqueness."

YOU SHOULD HAVE PRAYED ABOUT IT: PRIDE

"Hey, Harry, look at this investment opportunity I just got."

"What is it?"

"It says, 'You're a smart person. In fact, you're smarter than most people.' They're right about that, you know."

"Which is why you're going to put that come-on in the round file, right?"

"Throw it away? No way. Listen. 'Only a small number of particularly astute investors will be able to take advantage of this opportunity to get a yield on their investment of up to 1200 percent.' I'm one of those."

"*Up to* 1200 percent? and down to minus your entire investment. Toss it. It's a scam."

"Well, we can obviously see who wears the brains in this discussion. I'm going to invest $60,000. Because I'm brilliant."

"That's a lot of money. But education is expensive, they say."

"What are you talking about? I'm not going back to school. This is an investment."

†
📖

When pride comes, then comes dishonor,
But with the humble is wisdom.
—Proverbs 11:2 (NASB)

†
📖

Pride goes before destruction,
And a haughty spirit before stumbling.
—Proverbs 16:18 (NASB)

Greed. "Stock up now." "Collect them all." "Get what's yours." "Get rich quick." "Too much is not enough." "You can have it all."

YOU SHOULD HAVE PRAYED ABOUT IT: GREED

"Hey, K.C. You look worse than the trash heap of a car you're sitting in. What's the skinny? Yet another girlfriend dump you for a better looking guy?"

"No. I just lost all my cash."

"You lost it? How?"

"Well, I went to the grocery store to get some stuff, and a couple of guys in the parking lot—."

"Robbed you? Oh, K.C., that's evil."

"No, I actually robbed myself."

"Huh?"

"These guys said they had some very expensive speakers, extra—well the order was accidentally filled twice, and no one noticed, so they had these to sell under the table, so to speak."

"Out of the back of their van? This is beginning to smell."

"But the speakers were retail $2200 each they said, and they were selling them for $400 each."

"$2200 each, *they said*."

"Yeah, well, I talked them down to $220. One tenth of retail.

"But?"

"But when I got them home, they turned out to be thin plywood boxes with cheap, tiny little speakers behind the cloth grille."

"And since you basically agreed to buy what you thought was stolen property, you'd be embarrassed to call the cops and tell them you got scammed."

"But they were such a good deal."

✝
📖

But those who want to get rich fall into temptation and a snare and many foolish and harmful desires which plunge men into ruin and destruction. For the love of money is a root of all sorts of evil, and some by longing for it have wandered away from the faith and pierced themselves with many griefs.

— 1 Timothy 6:9-10 (NASB)

Anger. "Get revenge now." "Kick them in the teeth." "Lose control." "You don't have to take that." "Give him a piece of your mind."

YOU SHOULD HAVE PRAYED ABOUT IT: ANGER

"Why, Wanda. What are you doing here at the grocery store midmorning? Do you have the day off from work?"

"You might say that, Madge. I just got fired."

"Oh, no! What happened?"

"Well, this morning I was pulling onto 4ᵗʰ Street near the plant, when this idiot cuts me off and almost makes me crash into the car next to me."

"Oh, that's awful. But—."

"And then he pulls into the drive through lane at Koffee King. That made my blood boil."

"But what does this have to do with your getting fired?"

"Well, I pulled in behind the guy and started honking my horn with long blasts and showing him a few gestures to make the point."

"Oh, Wanda."

"He got out of his car and came over to me, and I acquainted him with some of my special vocabulary that I reserve for shouting at idiots."

"But I still don't—."

"Long story less long. When I got to work and attended the morning planning meeting, guess—."

"No! He was there?"

"A visit by the new regional manager."

"Oh, dear Wanda. I'm so sorry for you."

"How could I have known?"

✝

Do not be eager in your heart to be angry,
For anger resides in the bosom of fools.
—Ecclesiastes 7:9 (NASB)

Gluttony. "Welcome to the all-you-can-eat buffet." "Our desserts are a foot tall." "Supersize it."

YOU SHOULD HAVE PRAYED ABOUT IT: GLUTTONY

"Hey there, Malo. I guess you heard about Gordo."

"His funeral? Yeah. What I don't understand is why it cost $45,000 to bury him."

"Yeah, that's a lot. But think. There was the triple plots they had to buy, plus the piano-case-sized casket, plus the crane to lift the casket, and the large panel truck to move the casket to the cemetery."

"But forty-five grand. That's steep."

"And Madge, his widow, has those two anorexic daughters to take care of."

"Yeah. Sad. Hey, are you up for the Grand Buffet for lunch today? I hear they're having an eating contest."

"Count on it."

✝
📖

One of themselves, a prophet of their own, said, "Cretans are always liars, evil beasts, lazy gluttons."
—Titus 1:12 (NASB)

Lust. "Gives your mouth sex appeal." "Get Lucky tonight." Some perfume names: *Lush Lust; Dirty, Sexy, Wilde; Midnight Heat; Tabu.*

YOU SHOULD HAVE PRAYED ABOUT IT: LUST

"Hey, Tony. You got a package."

"Thanks, Wes. Oh, boy. Ladies, here I come. And you can't resist me."

"So what's in the package?"

"It's my new cologne. It has a secret chemical in it that will make me irresistible to women."

"And wherever did you find that?"

"It was in an ad in the back of a magazine. It said, 'One whiff of this formula and any woman will be putty in your hands.' It's a secret, miracle formula. And it's guaranteed to get women."

"And what did this miracle set you back?"

"Well, it cost $180, but if it works, it's worth it. There's enough applications in this half-ounce bottle to get a ton of babes."

"A half ounce for $180?"

"Plus shipping."

"Wouldn't it be better if you tried to find a girl who can think? She might be able to help you out."

"Think? Who cares about thinking?"

✝
📖

And if He rescued righteous Lot, oppressed by the sensual conduct of unprincipled men . . . then the Lord knows how to rescue the godly from temptation, and to keep the unrighteous under punishment for the day of judgment, and especially those who indulge the flesh in its corrupt desires and despise authority.

—2 Peter 2:7a, 9-10 (NASB)

Envy. "Your neighbors will envy your lawn when you use this fertilizer." "You'll be the envy of your friends in this new car."

YOU SHOULD HAVE PRAYED ABOUT IT: ENVY

"Brad, am I cute?"

"Of course, Emi. You're gorgeous."

"Am I as cute as Nicole?"

"Well, you're cute in a different way. Can't really be compared."

"So what you're really saying is I'm ugly."

"No, I—."

"I wish I were as cute as Nicole. And looked the way Janet looks in a sweater. And had Jennifer's legs. And Tanya's—."

"But if you had all that, then I wouldn't be your boyfriend."

"Why not?"

"Jordan would be. Cute calls to cute, don't you know. You'd drop me like a spider you mistook for — ."

"But Jordan is a jerk. He's a player."

"But he's a cute jerk of a player."

"Well, anyway, whatever boyfriend I ended up with, I still wish I could be really cute."

✝
📖

For from within, out of the heart of men, proceed the evil thoughts, fornications, thefts, murders, adulteries, deeds of coveting and wickedness, as well as deceit, sensuality, envy, slander, pride and foolishness. All these evil things proceed from within and defile the man.

— Mark 7:21-23 (NASB)

✝
📖

Therefore, putting aside all malice and all deceit and hypocrisy and envy and all slander, like newborn babies, long for the pure milk of the word, so that by it you may grow in respect to salvation, if you have tasted the kindness of the Lord.

— 1 Peter 2:1-3 (NASB)

✝
📖

Do not want anything that belongs to someone else. Don't want anyone's house, wife or husband, slaves, oxen, donkeys or anything else.

— Exodus 20:17 (CEV)

Sloth. "Pretend you're working." "Why do it today when you can do it tomorrow?" "Just relax."

"Honey? Honey! HONEY!"

"What is it, Wayne?"

"Bring me some triple A batteries. The remote is dead."

"Well, you've been watching TV for three days straight. It's no wonder the batteries are out."

"Well, duh. That's why I need some. Come on and bring them here."

"There are extra batteries in the drawer by the sofa, not three feet away from you. And I'm all the way across the room. Does that suggest anything to you?"

"Just skip the lecture and bring the batteries. And while you're at it, I need another soda and more popcorn."

"You also need a job."

"I've told you, working makes me tired. Besides, Bess, you earn enough to keep us okay."

"Why don't you see if there's a greeter's job at one of those super stores? That should be easy work."

"Oh, that reminds me. After you cook dinner and do the dishes, I need you to wash my car. I'm going into town tomorrow. There's a great new movie playing."

"I knew I should have prayed when I was looking for a husband."

"What are you talking about, woman? You've got a husband. Me. Remember?"

"Yes. Only too well."

"Huh? Darn remote. Where's those batteries?"

✝
📖

Whatever you do, do your work heartily, as for the Lord rather than for men.

—Colossians 3:23 (NASB)

✝

📖

A little sleep, a little slumber,
A little folding of the hands to rest,
Then your poverty will come as a robber
And your want like an armed man.
                              —Proverbs 24:33-34 (NASB)

Temptations are everywhere. The best way to fight them is to avoid them. Pray to be delivered from temptations, and when that is not possible, pray to be strong and resist them.

So long as we live in this world we cannot escape suffering and temptation. . . . Everyone, therefore, must guard against temptation and must watch in prayer lest the devil, who never sleeps but goes about seeking whom he may devour, find occasion to deceive him. No one is so perfect or so holy but he is sometimes tempted; man cannot be altogether free from temptation.
    —Thomas a Kempis, *The Imitation of Christ*, 1.13

☙ 🕊 ❧

A PRAYER TO RESIST TEMPTATION

Lord, you know my frailty, how my thoughts and sometimes my deeds go astray into sin. Only you and I know how rebellious my heart can sometimes be. So, the first thing I ask of you is that you keep temptations of every evil kind away from me, because I'm afraid that if I see them, I will be weak. And there's the reason for my second request, that if I encounter a temptation, you will give me the strength to resist it successfully, and the determination to walk away from it. Thank you so much for loving me enough to keep me from those spiritual mud puddles, and for washing me off when I fall in. I praise you in Jesus' name. Amen.

To overcome defensiveness.

Read a dozen books on relationships or interpersonal communication and all of them will warn you against defensiveness—the temptation to lash back in self-defense when blamed for something during an argument. Defensiveness, which amounts to blaming the person who is blaming you, always makes things worse rather than better. And yet our righteous indignation (or is it our pride?) at being blamed for something unjustly—and worse, by the person who is really at fault—makes the temptation to counterattack almost irresistible. Clearly, we need God's help here.

∽ 🕊 ∾
A PRAYER TO OVERCOME DEFENSIVENESS

Dear Lord, you know what has just happened. [Someone] is upset with me and is blaming me for the situation. Worse, they are acting immature about it and, to my thinking, making more of it than it deserves. You know, Lord, how sorely tempted I am to fight back and show them they're wrong or at least tell them to grow up and get over it. That's why I come to you. Please help me to guard my tongue, to resist making counterattacks or defensive excuses, and instead to say the words that will heal and not say the words that will hurt. Please don't let my pride or my ego get the better of me. Make me the peacemaker in this and guide my words. Thank you so very much. In Jesus' name. Amen.

For spiritual renewal.

Perhaps the most disturbing phenomenon encountered by new Christians is the arrival of a spiritual dry time. After a long time when the believer feels so close to God, a spiritual desert arrives, when the believer feels that the closeness has diminished. It is not unusual for those experiencing this dry period for the first time to feel distressed or even frightened. "Am I losing my faith?" they wonder.

The good news is, these times are known by many new and old believers alike, who understand that spiritual feelings sometimes diminish seemingly on their own accord, and that they return in the same way.

But if you begin to feel spiritually dry, you don't need to wait for spontaneous refreshing. Turn to prayer and ask God for the living water that can renew you. There's no better way to refocus your outlook when you've been distracted by the busyness of life.

৪০ 🕊 ೞ

A PRAYER FOR SPIRITUAL RENEWAL

Dear Lord, I'm not feeling as close to you as I once did, or as I know I ought to. My heart and soul seem to be dry and unexcited for the things of God, when I know I should be rejoicing in you and all that you do for me. Thank you for continuing to love me, even when my heart cools for a period.

Lord, please restore my passion for you. Send me a special visit from your Holy Spirit to rekindle the fires of love for you. Help me to feel your presence. I know you are there and I want to come close to you again.

Please grant me patience and trust to persevere through this waterless journey until it pleases you to

refresh my soul with your eternal living water. In Jesus' name I pray. Amen.

ᔥ 🕊 ᔐ
ANOTHER PRAYER FOR SPIRITUAL RENEWAL

God, I come to you feeling far away, as if somehow
we are not close the way we used to be. I feel spiritually dry. Even your word doesn't come alive and
speak to me the way it always did. I know that times
like this happen to many believers; and I also know
that those times pass and the dry ground soaks up
the new living water. But in the meantime, I feel sad.
Please refresh my spirit, dear God. May your Spirit
flood into my spirit and water my parched soul.
Help me to feel your presence and once again to
know that you are with me. If this feeling was
caused by a sin I have committed, please forgive me
and keep me from it. Thank you, Lord, for your un-
failing love. I ask your help in Jesus' name. Amen.

✝
📖

God, create a pure heart in me, and make my spirit
strong again.

—Psalm 51:10 (ERV)

To confess sin.

When we sin, why should we pray about it? After
all, God already knows we've sinned. And so do we.
So why confess? There are several reasons.

- God wants us to acknowledge that we did indeed sin. We are not to ignore it or sweep it
  under the rug.
- God wants us to repent of the sin and ask for
  forgiveness, humbling ourselves before him in
  contrition.

- God wants us to be forgiven, regain the right path, and ask for the necessary strength so that we will not sin again.

✝
📖

I acknowledged my sin to You, And my iniquity I did not hide; I said, "I will confess my transgressions to the Lord"; And You forgave the guilt of my sin. Selah. Therefore, let everyone who is godly pray to You in a time when You may be found. . . .
—Psalm 32:5-6a (NASB)

✝
📖

Therefore, confess your sins to one another.
—James 5:16a (NASB)

🕊

A PRAYER TO CONFESS SIN

Well, dear God, you know I've messed up again. I don't know what gets into me or why I'm so weak, but I am sorry for giving in to sin. Please forgive me. Please give me increased strength and willpower to resist the temptation in the future. Again, I'm sorry I have disappointed you and disgusted myself. May your hand of mercy and the blood of Christ be granted to me for forgiveness. Thank you, my loving Lord. In Jesus' name. Amen.

Acknowledging our failures to God is the first step in gaining forgiveness, forgiving others, and forgiving ourselves.

✝
📖

My little children, I am writing these things to you so that you may not sin. And if anyone sins, we have an Advocate with the Father, Jesus Christ the righteous; and He Himself is the propitiation for our sins; and not for ours only, but also for those of the whole world.

—1 John 2:1-2 (NASB)

To make requests.

In case you haven't ever noticed, the prayer that Jesus gave to his disciples as a model contains seven requests, three of them for others (God) and four of them for the person praying. So our model reveals that it is perfectly fine to pray for ourselves. The Lord knows we need food and forgiveness, and protection from ourselves and the evil one. So, you might say that the prayer Jesus taught us is 57% self-concerned.

This means that we are indeed to pray for ourselves and our needs and wants.

✝
📖

Be anxious for nothing, but in everything by prayer and supplication with thanksgiving let your requests be made known to God.

—Philippians 4:6 (NASB)

℘ 🕊 ℂ
A PRAYER TO MAKE A REQUEST

I thank you, dear Lord, for welcoming us to pray to you at any time, to ask for our needs. We recognize you as the source of all good things and as the one who has the power to supply our wants and remedy our hurts. I now come to you, O Lord, at your invitation, to ask once again for your help. I need your power and providing in this [issue]. If it pleases you, may it be your will to work this out according to my request and so that it can be to your glory. Do your will in this and in all things. In Jesus' name I pray. Amen.

ဆ 🕊 ၣ

A PRAYER FOR A SAFE JOURNEY

O Lord, I am grateful that you are sovereign over all the earth and its every event. You have the power to protect us from the evils of life. I therefore come to you now to ask that you will be with me in this coming journey, and if it is your will, that you will keep me safe through every part of it. Please make all the connections and pieces of this trip occur as scheduled, and bring me to the end of the journey safely and on time. In Jesus' name I thank you. Amen.

✝
📖

You will seek Me and find Me when you search for Me with all your heart.

—Jeremiah 29:13 (NASB)

To persuade God.

What do you think is the most powerful way God can demonstrate his care for his children who follow Jesus and at the same time demonstrate the almost frightening power of prayer? Are you aware that prayer is so powerful that it can influence God not only to take an action but to change his mind? Yes, believers can alter the course of history by prayer. Consider these examples:

Hezekiah's Answered Prayer

King Hezekiah learns through Isaiah that his illness is going to be terminal:

✝
📖

In those days Hezekiah became mortally ill. And Isaiah the prophet the son of Amoz came to him and said to him, "Thus says the LORD, 'Set your house in order, for you shall die and not live.'"
— 2 Kings 20:1 (NASB)

But Hezekiah turns to the Lord in prayer and groans for mercy:

✝
📖

Then he turned his face to the wall and prayed to the LORD, saying, "Remember now, O LORD, I beseech You, how I have walked before You in truth and with a whole heart and have done what is good in Your sight." And Hezekiah wept bitterly.
— 2 Kings 20:2-3 (NASB)

God is moved by this humble entreaty and changes his mind about Hezekiah's illness being fatal:

✝
📖

Before Isaiah had gone out of the middle court, the word of the LORD came to him, saying, "Return and say to Hezekiah the leader of My people, 'Thus says the LORD, the God of your father David, "I have heard your prayer, I have seen your tears; behold, I will heal you. On the third day you shall go up to the house of the LORD."'"
— 2 Kings 20:4-5 (NASB)

And not only will the king recover enough in three days to enter the house of the Lord, but God grants him several additional blessings:

✝
📖

I will add fifteen years to your life, and I will deliver you and this city from the hand of the king of Assyria; and I will defend this city for My own sake and for My servant David's sake.
— 2 Kings 20:6 (NASB)

Talk about the power of prayer! God does listen to our prayers, and considers our requests:

✝
📖

The effective prayer of a righteous man can accomplish much.
— James 5:16b (NASB)

Amos' Answered Prayer
Another example of God's listening to prayer and responding to it is found in the book of Amos, where the Lord reveals to Amos, through a vision, his plans to visit destruction on Israel for its sin:

✝
📖

Thus the Lord GOD showed me, and behold, He was forming a locust-swarm when the spring crop began to sprout. And behold, the spring crop was after the king's mowing.
— Amos 7:1 (NASB)

But Amos intercedes and prays that the Lord will have mercy, and the Lord relents:

✝

📖

And it came about, when it had finished eating the vegetation of the land, that I said, "Lord GOD, please pardon! How can Jacob stand, For he is small?" The LORD changed His mind about this. "It shall not be," said the LORD.

—Amos 7:2-3 (NASB)

Amos' entreaty also persuades the Lord not to visit fire on Israel:

✝

📖

Thus the Lord GOD showed me, and behold, the Lord GOD was calling to contend with them by fire, and it consumed the great deep and began to consume the farm land. Then I said, "Lord GOD, please stop! How can Jacob stand, for he is small?" The LORD changed His mind about this. "This too shall not be," said the Lord GOD.

—Amos 7:4-6 (NASB)

Moses' Answered Prayer

As a final example, in Exodus chapter 32, the Lord tells Moses that he is out of patience with Israel and is going to destroy the people:

✝

📖

The LORD said to Moses, "I have seen this people, and behold, they are an obstinate people. Now then let Me alone, that My anger may burn against them and that I may destroy them; and I will make of you a great nation."

—Exodus 32:9-10 (NASB)

Moses cares for his people, and doesn't want to accept God's offer. Instead, he engages in an extended argument with God:

✝
📖

Then Moses entreated the LORD his God, and said, "O LORD, why does Your anger burn against Your people whom You have brought out from the land of Egypt with great power and with a mighty hand? Why should the Egyptians speak, saying, 'With evil intent He brought them out to kill them in the mountains and to destroy them from the face of the earth'?"

— Exodus 32:11-12a (NASB)

Moses asks specifically for God to change his mind and spare his people:

✝
📖

"Turn from Your burning anger and change Your mind about doing harm to Your people. Remember Abraham, Isaac, and Israel, Your servants to whom You swore by Yourself, and said to them, 'I will multiply your descendants as the stars of the heavens, and all this land of which I have spoken I will give to your descendants, and they shall inherit it forever.'"

— Exodus 32:12b-13 (NASB)

And the Lord answers Moses' prayer and agrees not to destroy Israel, once again showing that prayer does have an effect on God's actions toward his children:

✝
📖
So the LORD changed His mind about the harm
which He said He would do to His people.
—Exodus 32:9-14 (NASB)

A theological note.

If you're worried about the theology of how an
omniscient God can change his mind, the answer is
that, even though God knows the future, our prayers
can still affect it. Although we should always pray for
God's will, we are told to ask for our needs, and that
they will conform to his preferential or at least his
permissive will. (See Chapter 13: Three Aspects of
God's Will.) One of the major purposes of prayer is to
show God what really matters to us and to influence
his actions accordingly.

It would indeed be a strange dispensation if we
were asked to "pray without ceasing" (1 Thessalonians
5:17), and yet to be told that our prayers would have
no effect. We pray because we can influence God's actions.

Look at a few of the many Scriptures that reflect
this point: "Ask of Me" (Psalm 2:8), "Good things to
those who ask him" (Matthew 7:11), "Ask for in prayer" (Matthew 21:22), "Ask the Father" (John 15:16),
"Ask God" (James 1:5), "Ask anything according to his
will" (1 John 5:14).

✝
📖
You will call to Me and come and pray to Me, and I
will listen to you.
—Jeremiah 29:12 (NASB)

ಬ 🕊 ಏ

A PRAYER FOR GOD'S GRACE

My dear Lord, it seems as if things I don't like and don't want are coming my way at a faster and faster pace. I don't know whether this is your will or whether I'm just on the receiving end of a set of harmful coincidences. Whatever the case, I come to you humbly and submissively, asking that you will pour out your grace on me and remedy these things that are hurting me. Deliver me, O Lord, not because I deserve it but for the sake of your precious son, Jesus. If it pleases you, may it be your will to help me and save me from these things. I ask and thank you in the name of Jesus. Amen.

Speaking to his children who live in every era and every nation, the Lord promises to help those who love and follow him:

✝
📖

I will bless you with a future filled with hope—a future of success, not of suffering.
—Jeremiah 29:11 (CEV)

To find God.

Perhaps you are reading this book out of curiosity about prayer and those who practice it, but you aren't sure about the whole enterprise. There is a prayer for you. If you think there is the possibility that roses and crystals and panda bears and tropical plants were actually designed as they certainly appear to be, or if you already acknowledge that there must be something divine—yes, call him God—then why not take the next step and seek him out?

Here is a prayer that will help you.

ঞ 🕊 প্র
A PRAYER TO FIND GOD

This prayer is addressed to the God who created the heavens and the earth, and everything in them. For that God is God. If you are there, if you are real, I ask that you reveal yourself to me. Others have told me that you have revealed yourself through the Bible. I will be reading it to see if that is true. Thank you and I hope to find you soon.

Why this prayer? The Bible tells us that the beauty of the creation gives evidence for God, so it is an obvious place to begin.

✝
📖
The heavens proclaim the glory of God.
The skies display His craftsmanship.
　　　　　　　　—Psalm 19:1 (NLT)

God's sense of beauty, design, esthetics, art, and even sense of humor (have you looked at some of the insects on this planet?) can all be discerned by a careful examination of the natural world.

✝
📖
For ever since the world was created, people have seen the earth and sky. Through everything God made, they can clearly see His invisible qualities— His eternal power and divine nature. So they have no excuse for not knowing God.
　　　　　　　　—Romans 1:20 (NLT)

Indeed, the God question is the most important question anyone can ask because the answer will affect every decision and behavior of your life, and, if we Christians are to be believed, it will affect you for eternity.

In his book, *Pensees*, Blaise Pascal discusses those who aren't interested in Christianity. He explains why non-interest is an untenable position:

> Let them recognize that there are only two kinds of person whom we can describe as reasonable: Those who serve God with all their heart because they have found him, and those who seek him with all their heart because they have not found him.
>
> — *Pensees* 11

To be saved.

If you have led someone to Christ, or if you yourself have just placed your faith in Jesus, that new belief should begin with a prayer. Think of it as the oath of office or the club initiation declaration of loyalty. In this case, the new Christian makes a confession of sin and a pledge to follow Jesus. There are many of these so-called sinner's prayers. Here is one more.

ഔ 🕊 ൡ

A PRAYER FOR SALVATION

God, I admit that I haven't done a very good job trying to live by my own rules, which I too often didn't even follow. I also admit that when I used to say I thought I was good, I was speaking foolishly. God, I know that I'm a sinner, and I know that I can't buy my way into heaven with money or good deeds. But I do want to go to heaven when I die, to live forever in your kingdom because you are a loving and caring God. So I now put my belief, my faith, my trust in Jesus Christ, who died to cover my sins. And I thank you for the gift of eternal life. I want not only to believe as a Christian, but to live as a Christian, following the teachings of Jesus. Please take over the rule of my life and guide me through the future until the day you call me home. I ask these things in the name of Jesus, my Lord and Savior. Amen.

To obey God's command.

A final reason to pray is that God commands us to pray. He wants us to communicate with him because he knows we are easily distracted and easily led astray. The more we pray, the firmer and clearer will be our relationship with our creator and Lord.

†
📖

Therefore I want the men in every place to pray, lifting up holy hands, without wrath and dissension.
—1 Timothy 2:8 (NASB)

☙ 🕊 ❧
A PRAYER TO ANSWER GOD'S REQUEST

Dear Lord, I come to you with thanksgiving that you have told us to come to you in prayer, to praise and to ask, to thank and to worship. Thank you for being always available to listen to my heart and to consider my needs. Please let your Holy Spirit give me the words to say and to help me to be clear about my priorities. Forgive me for my sins and put me back on the path of virtue and obedience to your will. Keep me close, O Lord, and guide my ways. In Jesus' name. Amen.

ಐ 🕊 ೞ

ANOTHER PRAYER TO ANSWER GOD'S REQUEST

I come to you, dear Lord, for once without an urgent, specific need. I come into your presence because your word tells us that we are to pray to you with praises, thanksgivings, and requests.

So I gladly praise you for your goodness and guidance and love. I thank you with all my heart for your grace and generosity. And my request is that you will help me to love and serve you better each day. May I model my savior Jesus in all my words and actions. In his name I pray. Amen.

✠✠✠

Chapter 3 Questions for Thought and Discussion

1. Name three of the example prayers in this chapter that you find most relevant, effective, or useful in your own life. Explain why.
2. Name three of the example prayers in this chapter that you find least relevant, effective, or useful in your own life. Explain why.
3. Were any of the example prayers in this chapter covering a subject or issue you had not thought to bring to God in prayer? Explain why or why not.

Chapter 3 Activities

1. Think of a type of prayer missing from the list in this chapter and write a prayer covering that issue or theme.
2. Choose seven of the prayers from this chapter and pray one with your family each day for a week. Discuss your responses or reactions with each other.

3. Choose three categories from those discussed in this chapter and write your own prayers reflecting the theme.

Chapter 3 Group Activity

1. Discuss the concept of changing God's mind. Can you find Scripture verses that weigh in on either side? How can God be constant and unchanging and yet change his mind in answer to prayer? How can God change his mind in light of 1 Samuel 15:29, Psalm 15:4, Psalm 55:19, Psalm 110:4, Jeremiah 4:28, and Malachi 3:6?

(Hint: Must God sometimes need to change his actions in order to be unchangingly consistent when people change their actions? For example, see Deuteronomy 30:15-20.)

4

What to Ask of God

Prayer is launching out the heart toward God.
— Therese of Lisieux

In the last chapter we looked at reasons we should pray. Some of these reasons involve asking God for something. That something can include healing (physical or emotional), protection, guidance, help, forgiveness, strength or courage (to engage or to resist), outcomes (peace, a prosperous trip, an answer to a question), and so on. And, of course, some prayers are requests for material goods such as houses or cars. Because many of our prayers involve making requests, and because sometimes this kind of prayer can be misunderstood, a separate chapter seems appropriate.

Is asking for stuff selfish?

One criticism sometimes offered about asking God to do things is that it's selfish, since we almost always ask for things for ourselves. Remember, however, that when Jesus taught the disciples how to pray, his model prayer contained two praises and seven requests, including a request for daily food.

ᔆᵒ 🕊 ᙅᴙ

A PRAYER FOR MATERIAL GOODS

Dear Father in heaven, I come to you with a material need. Our [item] no longer works and cannot be repaired, and we need a replacement. You know our limited resources, O Lord, and you know how expensive [items] are. I ask for your guidance in finding a replacement and for your grace in helping us somehow to afford it. Please bless us spiritually as well as materially through this request. May your answer be in accordance with your will. In Jesus' name. Amen.

Fido versus world peace.

Because God is so mighty, and because there are needs of such monumental size, some people wonder if it's wrong to pray for small, even tiny things. Should we, in other words, spend our prayer time asking the Lord to bring about world peace rather than healing our little doggie's bleeding toenail?

The answer is, We should pray for both the doggie and world peace. Nothing is too small to bring to the Lord, if it is important to us. Don't be embarrassed to bring your dandruff or your cousin's smoking habit before God and ask for his help.

Remember the discussion of emergent prayers? It's perfectly fine—desirable, in fact—to pray for a good parking space, a safe journey, an on-time arrival, a low price at the gas station, or the item you want being in stock when you get to the store. The reason for this is not that you turn God into your butler or vending machine (see Chapter 6).

The reason for asking for small blessings is that every such prayer brings God and his presence to your mind, together with the growing understanding of how dependent you are on him and how gracious he is to you.

In *The Practice of the Presence of God*, Brother Lawrence says that

> we should establish ourselves in the presence of God, talking always with him.
>
> — First Conversation

ᘓ 🕊 ᘖ

A PRAYER FOR GOD'S GUIDANCE

Thank you, dear Lord, for being my God and my savior. I pray that you will be with me throughout the day, guiding me in all that I do, say, and think. If you have planned an appointment for me with a stranger, help me to model Christ in my attitude and actions, and give me the words to say that will be impactful in such a way that will lead the person to you. As ever, Lord, show me the path and help me to walk it with joy and competence. In the name of Jesus. Amen.

ᘓ 🕊 ᘖ

A PRAYER FOR SOMETHING SMALL

Dear Lord, please help me make this casserole to turn out well. As you know, the last time I forgot to add one of the main ingredients. Give me presence of mind and guide my hands as I prepare this. Thank you very much. In the name of Jesus. Amen.

Solomon's preference for wisdom over wealth.

When God asked young king Solomon what he wanted, in an "ask me anything" offer, Solomon asked for the gift of discernment.

✝
📖

God said to him, "Because you have asked this thing and have not asked for yourself long life, nor have asked riches for yourself, nor have you asked for the life of your enemies, but have asked for yourself discernment to understand justice, behold, I have done according to your words. Behold, I have given you a wise and discerning heart, so that there has been no one like you before you, nor shall one like you arise after you. I have also given you what you have not asked, both riches and honor, so that there will not be any among the kings like you all your days.

—1 Kings 3:11-13 (NASB)

This should be a model for us. We should offer prayers that reflect the true purpose of our lives and our desire to achieve that purpose: Our purpose is not to live large, eat gourmet meals, and consume products; it is to improve ourselves and serve others.

We should pray, then, for personal spiritual growth, guidance in making decisions, wisdom, understanding, compassion, a changed heart, and the ability to forgive more easily.

And don't forget to pray that you will know, and love, and live out God's preferred will for your life and the lives of those in your care.

Remember, however, to include in your prayers requests that will have a larger impact—petitions whose accomplishment would help remedy the damage from the Fall, or that will help you and others grow and mature in Christ.

✝
📖

Devote yourselves to prayer, keeping alert in it with an attitude of thanksgiving.
—Colossians 4:2-3a (NASB)

ഇ 🕊 ഷ
A PRAYER FOR INNER GROWTH

Lord, you know how much I'm overly obsessed about the details of life, always getting ready for an appointment, going shopping, meeting a friend, doing my work. It seems as if I hardly have time to pray. Help me, Lord, to "be still and know that you are God." Grant me not just peace of heart, but spiritual growth, drawing ever closer to you, worshipping you. Help me to think about the things of God. Help me to remember that I'm here to please and serve you and not to indulge myself or just take up space. Indeed, dear Lord, please give me wisdom, so that I can understand my purpose, other people, and especially you and your will for my life. I thank you so very much. In the name of the Lord Jesus. Amen.

Praying for others.

You don't need to have a God's eye view of the earth to know that there is a tremendous amount of human suffering and need in the world. A major use of our prayer time should always be as intercessors for others. Poverty, disease, disasters, and death are widespread, and the victims of these evils need our prayers.

We should begin our focus on others in our prayer life by praying for our family members and friends. I think everyone needs emotional support and encouragement, and we all can certainly use guidance in our decision making. Pray that the young members of the family will grow in maturity, the middle members in decision making, and the older members in better health.

&ᛦᏙᛦ Ꙉ

A PRAYER FOR HEALING

Dear Lord, you are the great healer of our souls, cleansing them from the filth of sin and making them well through your blood. I pray now that if it might be your will, you will heal [person] of [condition]. May it please you to do this work of healing out of your grace and goodness, and not because we pretend to deserve it. And if it is not your will to heal [person] at this time, help [him / her] to bear this [condition / disease / illness] with courage and trust in you. And healing or not, may you be glorified in everything. Thank you for your love. In Jesus' name. Amen.

&ᛦᏙᛦ Ꙉ

A PRAYER FOR THE WORLD

Dear God, this is such a corrupt, selfish, and sinful world that it's no wonder things are so bad. And yet this is also a deeply hurting world, with so many lost or misguided souls. Please have mercy on those who have been led astray. Send your Holy Spirit to work in both the hard hearts and the suffering hearts of all those who need to be redeemed from the Evil One. Place your mantle of grace on every continent and raise up believers who can plant the seeds of revival, so that nations can return to you and exalt you. Renew and refresh the faith of those who have wandered or cooled, and set aflame the hearts of many others as they see your truth and share it with others. Thank you so very much, our dear Lord. We ask these things in the name of Jesus. Amen.

For additional discussion about praying for others, see Chapter 12 on intercessory prayer.

Praying for everyone and everything.

Here, someone might ask, "Because there is so much need in the world and so many people who need prayer, is it okay to pray for a whole laundry list of people and things?"

A laundry-list prayer goes something like this:

ೞ 🕊 ಚ
A PRAYER FOR EVERYONE AND EVERYTHING

God bless Tom and Jane and Bill and Edna's foot and Nick's job and Fran and the Smith's car and the big game and send a cure for cancer and bring about world peace. Amen.

Is it all right to pray this way? An answer is suggested by two Scriptures. First, James tells us that in order to be effective, our prayers should be heartfelt and sincere and earnest.

✝

📖

The urgent request of a righteous person is very powerful in its effect. Elijah was a man with a nature like ours; yet he prayed earnestly that it would not rain, and for three years and six months it did not rain on the land.

—James 5:16b-17 (HCSB)

Now, it might be argued that laundry-list prayers like the one above could conceivably be heartfelt and earnest. However, laundry-list prayers tend to be repeated at least daily, and such a frequent repetition (like the Pledge of Allegiance or the Scout's Oath) tends to result in a mental autopilot, where the praying person isn't even paying attention to the prayer, much less communing with its recipient.

And Jesus tells us that haranguing God is not necessary. He hears you. There's no need to risk just going through the motions with a repetitive, wooden prayer.

✝

📖

And when you pray, don't be like the people who don't know God. They say the same things again and again. They think that if they say it enough, their god will hear them.

—Matthew 6:7 (ERV)

This doesn't mean that you should pray for something only once or twice. Certainly, you should pray regularly—and earnestly—for the things most important to you. The key is to be attentive, focused, and intentional whenever you pray. If you are a laundry-list prayer, here are some suggestions:

Divide your list of recipients into parts, and pray for one part each day or each week.

Take a few moments for each object of your prayer and think about the person or situation, so that you can pray with focused concern. Let the need resonate in your heart and mind as you pray for it.

Change the words you use to pray for a given person or situation so that there will be freshness in your thoughts and so you can avoid robot praying.

Wait until it occurs to you to pray for someone or something, and then offer a brief request: "And Lord, please do heal Uncle Ned of his cancer. According to your will. Amen."

In sum, then, it's not that God can't handle the data dump; it's an issue of human limitations. If, as we should, we want to think about and feel for those people and things we pray for, we ought to "pray more about less" at one time.

Asking for a miracle: No.

The question sometimes arises, "Should you ask God to perform a miracle or to do the humanly impossible?" There are two answers to this question, No and Yes. Let's consider.

First, do not pray that God will do anything that violates his nature. He won't do evil, lie, or wantonly kill your enemies.

Second, don't ask for anything that Scripture prohibits. See the Ten Commandments, for example. No, he won't give you your neighbor's spouse.

Third, remember that the bigger the miracle you are asking for, the more likely other people might be anxiously praying for the opposite. I pray for rain; you pray for fair weather. I pray that candidate X will win; you pray that candidate Y will win. And don't even get me started about all those praying to win the lottery.

Lastly, avoid asking God to violate the laws of physics or space-time. He is unlikely to take you back to last Tuesday so you can stop yourself from engaging in that hurtful argument.

Asking for a miracle: Yes.

There are many instances, both Biblical and historical, of miraculous healings, escapes, victories, and blessings. With prayer, "impossible" problems have been solved, battles have been won, and terminal patients have been healed.

✝
📖

Behold, I am the LORD, the God of all flesh; is anything too difficult for Me?

—Jeremiah 32:27 (NASB)

Indeed, God is a God of the impossible, a God of miracles. If it pleases him, he can stagger you with his power and sudden deliverance. If he can keep a trio of guys cool while their enemies are trying to cremate them in a furnace (see Daniel, chapter 3), he can be beyond what you can ever imagine (Ephesians 3:20). Don't worry if the answer to your prayer seems difficult. Nothing is too difficult for God.

ഔ 🕊 �
A PRAYER FOR A MIRACLE

Dear God, I come to you with a heavy heart and a failing hope. In spite of all the human treatments, it seems certain that [person] is going to pass away soon from [condition]. Now, only you have the power to intervene and bring healing. So I ask you that, if you are willing, you will work the miracle necessary to heal [person], not for [his / her] sake, nor for my sake, but for your love of Jesus. Only you know the plans you have for [person], so I ask above all that you do your will. And if it pleases you to call [him / her] home now, may [his / her] passing into the kingdom be free from pain or suffering. I ask these things in the name of him who will eventually call us all into your kingdom, our Lord and savior, Jesus Christ. Amen.

Praying against evil.

Sometimes the question arises about whether it is appropriate to pray *against* some things or people as well as *for* things and people. The issue is especially in play when it comes to those who run oppressive dictatorships. There are in this world — and probably always will be — some viciously terrible dictators causing indescribable suffering to a large number of people. They are outright psychopaths whose most prominent personality trait seems to be pointless sadism. I don't know about you, but I am sorely tempted to pray that God will put them and their enablers on a bus and run it off a high cliff.

But that's not Biblical.

Scripture teaches us to take a very different approach. First, Paul tells us to pray for everyone, including all those in authority so that we can have peaceful lives. He doesn't distinguish between good and bad people in authority:

✝
📖

First of all, then, I urge that entreaties and prayers, petitions and thanksgivings, be made on behalf of all men, for kings and all who are in authority, so that we may lead a tranquil and quiet life in all godliness and dignity.

—1 Timothy 2:1-2 (NASB)

Next, we are to be subject to authority, because it has been appointed by God:

✝
📖

Every person is to be in subjection to the governing authorities. For there is no authority except from God, and those which exist are established by God.

—Romans 13:1 (NASB)

And God desires everyone—even evil dictators—to be saved:

✝
📖

This is good and acceptable in the sight of God our Savior, who desires all men to be saved and to come to the knowledge of the truth.

—1 Timothy 2:3-4 (NASB)

Even more pointedly, Jesus himself tells us to love our enemies:

✝
📖

You have heard that it was said, "You shall love your neighbor and hate your enemy." But I say to you, love your enemies and pray for those who persecute you, so that you may be sons of your

Father who is in heaven; for He causes His sun to
rise on the evil and the good, and sends rain on the
righteous and the unrighteous.
— Matthew 5:43-45 (NASB)

So, how do we pray about evil regimes? There are several possibilities. First, we can pray that God will
change their behavior: Praying that the leaders will
gain wisdom, insight, even the understanding that a
fair, just, moral rule makes the best government. Second, we can pray that God will change the hearts of the
leaders so that they can be saved. And third, yes, we
can ask for God to supply a new leader who will be
humane. Asking for regime change is completely acceptable as long as we don't ask God to kill the leaders
as part of the request.

ഈ 🕊 രു
A PRAYER TO END EVIL

Dear Lord, I come to you burdened by [country],
whose corrupt and evil leaders have left their people
in dire poverty even while those in charge plunder
the nation's resources. Lord, please work in the lives
of these leaders to soften their hearts, that they may
change their behavior and grow wise and good in
their governance. Open their eyes that they might
see the hunger and misery their people are suffering
and follow a path that will bring prosperity. Have
mercy on the people of [country], and deliver them.
I ask with thankfulness in Jesus' name. Amen.

Now, what if you have been praying this for a long
time? Then perhaps it's time to ask God to replace the
leadership. Don't ask for violence, but defer to God's
methods and timing. In Psalm 5, which is itself a model

prayer, David provides a good example of praying against evil people:

✝

📖

FROM PSALM 5

Every morning, Lord, I lay my gifts before you and look to you for help. And every morning you hear my prayers. . . . But by your great mercy, I can enter your house. I can worship in your holy Temple with fear and respect for you. Lord, show me your right way of living, and make it easy for me to follow. People are looking for my weaknesses, so show me how you want me to live.

My enemies never tell the truth. They only want to destroy people. Their words come from mouths that are like open graves. They use their lying tongues to deceive others. Punish them, God! Let them be caught in their own traps. They have turned against you, so punish them for their many crimes.

But let those who trust in you be happy forever. Protect and strengthen those who love your name. Lord, when you bless good people, you surround them with your love, like a large shield that protects them.

—Psalm 5:3, 7-12 (ERV)

Note here how David wisely asks for the What (punish the evil ones), but he does not ask for the How. That choice he leaves to God. We should do the same. God can always fit the right punishment to the crime in a way that will meet the needs of both retribution and reformation. Some people might need a substantial event before they will change their ways, while others might need only a little change in their personal weather.

ഇൗ 🕊 ൠ

A PRAYER FOR CHANGE

Dear God, the nation and the people of [country] have long suffered under a cruel government, and there seems to be no improvement coming. I pray that you will look upon that nation and its leaders, and if it is in your will, that you will deliver the country from its current leaders and replace them with good and just and even righteous people. You know what is best, O Lord, so may your will be done in this as with everything. Thank you for considering my request. In Jesus' name I pray. Amen.

If, as with every request, we remember to submit our askings to God's will, we will demonstrate our recognition that God knows best what to do. Our perspective is narrow; God's is infinite in every direction.

✢✢✢

Chapter 4 Questions for Thought and Discussion

1. Have you ever prayed for a miracle? Explain the circumstances. Was it for a large miracle or a small one? What was the result of your prayers?

2. How wide ranging are your typical prayers? Do you focus your requests or praises on yourself and your family? your relatives? your state? nation? the world? Do you typically pray mostly for individuals or for groups?

3. Have you ever prayed for an abstract personal need such as wisdom, maturity, knowledge, or friendliness? Did you take steps to provide a way for God to answer? What was the result?

Chapter 4 Activities

1. Make a list of half a dozen to ten prayer requests you have made and arrange them from smallest to largest. Examine the list and think about the breadth of your requests. Is there room at the small end or the large end for additional prayers?

2. Is your view of God or God's busyness keeping you from praying for some things at the small end?

3. Is your view of God's willingness, love, power, usual practice or some other characteristic keeping you from praying for some things on the large end?

Chapter 4 Group Activities

1. Take your list from question 1 under Activities and share it with the group. What is the smallest thing anyone in the group has prayed for? What is the largest thing? What answers did people receive?

2. Discuss as a group question 2 above under Activities.

3. Discuss as a group question 3 above under Activities.

5

Why Some Prayers Go Unanswered

To approach God, one should go straight to him, like a ball from a cannon.
— *John Vianney*

If you think deeply and consider adequately, read the Bible and pray respectfully, you'll understand well enough who God is and who you are in relation to him, and therefore you won't even need to read this chapter.

But just to be complete, I've included this discussion about why God rejects some prayers (which the person praying sees as an answer of No).

Praying without living a righteous life.

Yes, the Bible tells us that, while God can answer anyone's prayer, he usually listens to the prayer of the righteous, because they are striving to please him. God helps those who love him and strive to obey his rules. And loving God means more than a warm feeling toward him. Loving God means demonstrating that love through action—living in obedience to his rules. As it is sometimes said, love is a verb. Love is what you do, not just how you feel.

To put it briefly:

✝
📖

If you love Me, you will keep My commandments.
—John 14:15 (NASB)

Scripture is clear about this. Answered prayer is connected to an obedient lifestyle:

✝
📖

Beloved, if our heart does not condemn us, we have confidence before God; and whatever we ask we receive from Him, because we keep His command-ments and do the things that are pleasing in His sight.
—1 John 3:21-22 (NASB)

It's not just how deeply someone feels about a prayer request—or how often someone prays—that influences God; it's the righteous believer whom God hears:

✝
📖

The earnest prayer of a righteous person has great power and produces wonderful results.
—James 5:16b (NLT)

We too often forget that many of God's promises are contingent on our behavior. We can't just say we are Christians and expect our prayers to be answered if we continue to be disobedient to God's word. There are Scriptures from both testaments that support this.

✝

📖

If you obey the LORD, he will watch over you and answer your prayers.
                    —Psalm 34:15 (CEV)

✝

📖

In the same way, you husbands should live with your wives in an understanding way, since they are weaker than you. You should show them respect, because God gives them the same blessing he gives you—the grace of true life. Do this so that nothing will stop your prayers from being heard.
                    —1 Peter 3:7 (ERV)

All believers still sin on occasion. They are not the ones God ignores. He hears the prayers of those who strive for righteousness. The prayers of the hardened sinners—the wicked—are the prayers God puts into his cosmic shredder.

✝

📖

The sacrifice of the wicked is an abomination to the LORD,
But the prayer of the upright is His delight.
                    —Proverbs 15:8 (NASB)

✝

📖

The LORD is far from the wicked,
But He hears the prayer of the righteous.
                    —Proverbs 15:29 (NASB)

After all, God knows hypocrisy when he hears it. Those who don't care to follow the path God has laid out for them are not likely to be heard:

✝

📖

He who turns away his ear from listening to the law,
Even his prayer is an abomination.
—Proverbs 28:9 (NASB)

✝

📖

We know that God doesn't listen to sinners, but He
is ready to hear those who worship Him and do His
will.
—John 9:31 (NLT)

Wanting to have our prayers answered, then, is one
more incentive to live a good, faithful, holy, and righteous life. All of us need to examine how well we obey
God and his commandments.

✝

📖

For I am the LORD your God. Consecrate yourselves
therefore, and be holy, for I am holy.
—Leviticus 11:44a (NASB)

✝

📖

As obedient children, do not be conformed to the
former lusts which were yours in your ignorance,
but like the Holy One who called you, be holy
yourselves also in all your behavior; because it is
written, "You shall be holy, for I am holy."
—1 Peter 1:14-16 (NASB)

Sound impossible? With God's help and his mercy
for the many times we fail, we can ultimately succeed.

†
📖

For I can do everything through Christ, who gives me strength.

— Philippians 4:13 (NLT)

Telling God *how* rather than asking for *what*.

Sometimes people confuse *what* they want with *how* it should be delivered.

KNOW, HOW?

"Hello. Mr. McMurty? Joe from Joe's Appliance Repair. Nice to meet you. I understand you have a washing machine that isn't draining right."

"Yeah. It's in here. The water pump needs to be replaced. That will fix it."

"Well, let's just take a look. Usually on this model when you get poor or no drainage, either there is a lint clog or the drain solenoid has stopped working."

"The water pump needs to be replaced. Forget about lint and whatever that solenoid thing is."

"Uh, Okay. Let me see."

[Two hours later]

"All done, Mr. McMurty."

"Did you replace the water pump?"

"Yep, as you requested. And I cleaned out the lint clog that was the cause of the draining problem."

"What do I owe you?"

"Well, cleaning out the lint clog, with the service call, comes to $102. The water pump was $147 and an additional hour of labor to install it is $100, so your total bill is $349.

"Yikes. Why are repairs so expensive?"

Yes, I shrewdly told this clever story for a reason. And, yes, you guessed it. When you pray and ask God for something—the What—leave the How to him. He often has a better way of getting you what you want than you are thinking of. So if you find that you are praying for a How, and that prayer seems to be unanswered, look around to see if it was answered with a different How. Or revise your prayer and let God be God.

Asking with the wrong motives.

God listens to our voice when we ask for the What, When and Where. And he also listens to our heart for the Why.

†
📖
Man does not see what the LORD sees, for man sees what is visible, but the LORD sees the heart.
—1 Samuel 16:7b (HCSB)

Yes, God knows our motives when we pray, and if our motives are wrong (selfish, immoral, vengeful), he may refuse to honor our request, even if it is otherwise worthy.

†
📖
You desire and do not have. . . . You do not have because you do not ask. You ask and don't receive because you ask with wrong motives, so that you may spend it on your evil desires.
—James 4:2-3 (HCSB)

Trying to manipulate God.

It's just bad form to remind God about all you have done for him—helping the poor, praying for Aunt Biddy, taking the Pastor to lunch, resisting cheating on your taxes—with the implication that God therefore really should look favorably on your request.

Prayers like this are not a good idea for several reasons. First, God already knows all these things you've done, and second, you and God are not in a transactional relationship where you balance inputs with each other. Leave the quid-pro-quo relationships to business folks. Finally, the implication that "I've done something for you, so you owe me," is insulting even on a human level, so think how much more it is on a creature-to-creator level.

Oh, and fourth, prayers like this can sound as if you're trying to shame God into action. If you want something, forget your goodness laundry list. Just ask for what you want and leave it to God's will and his purposes. He can read your heart.

Now, I realize that some Biblical characters did nearly what I'm criticizing here. King Hezekiah did this when God told him he was going to die:

✝
📖

"Remember, O LORD, how I have always been faithful to You and have served You single-mindedly, always doing what pleases You." Then he broke down and wept bitterly.
—2 Kings 20:3 (NASB)

And as I mentioned elsewhere, God answered Hezekiah's prayer and gave him fifteen extra years of life. But for the reasons I've given, I wouldn't consider

Hezekiah as a model to use when praying for a personal need. Instead, I agree with Isaiah, that it is arrogant to boast about our righteous deeds, whether to God or anyone:

†
📖

We are all infected and impure with sin. When we display our righteous deeds, they are nothing but filthy rags. Like autumn leaves, we wither and fall, and our sins sweep us away like the wind.
—Isaiah 64:6 (NLT)

It seems to me that a humble approach to God is the better choice when asking for his help.

🕉 🕊 ೞ

THE BEGINNING OF A HUMBLE PRAYER FOR HELP

My dear Lord, I know I don't deserve your help in this. In spite of my attempts to live a good life, I realize that my good deeds pale in comparison to my sins. Please forgive me, and change my ways to ways that always please you. And not for my sake but for Jesus' sake, please consider my request. . . .

Trying to bribe God.

Too often, when some people face dire consequences, they attempt to bargain with God. A better term than *bargain* is *bribe*.

THE BARGAIN

"Jake? Is that you, uh, praying?"
"Yeah, Angie. Don't bother me."
"But—."
"Dear God up there in heaven, just do this one thing for me and I'll start going to church."

"Like that's going to happen."

"Shut up Angie. I'm praying. Oh Lord, Lord, Lord, you know what a scrape I'm in. Just get me out of it and I'll give money to the poor and to the church."

"Yeah, right."

"Didn't I tell you to shut up? Not you, God, that was for Angie. But, God, if you get me out of this, I'll never be bad again. I promise. Thanks. Amen."

"Jake, you're a riot. You think God is going to listen to you?"

"Why shouldn't he? Didn't you hear what I offered him?"

Take it straight: God cannot be bribed into answering your prayer. Love, money, promised behavior changes, the straight and narrow—don't even bother because he doesn't take bribes.

✝
📖

For the LORD your God is the God of gods and Lord of lords, the great, mighty, and awesome God, showing no partiality and taking no bribe.
— Deuteronomy 10:17 (NASB)

When you are facing a problem, large or small, chosen by you, imposed on you, or of your own making, go before the Lord and ask plainly for his help. Don't try to turn your request into a bargaining session.

If you're not a Christian, it is true that God reserves the right to make exceptions and answer a nonbeliever's request when it suits a heavenly purpose. But why risk it? If you truly want God's ear, change your life first—make friends with Jesus, follow him, obey him, accept his offer of salvation and live the Christian life. Then, ask away.

Trying to manipulate another person.

This type of prayer is prayed aloud, for the supposed benefit of someone participating in the prayer. You've probably heard this type.

GILT TRIP

"Thank you, Alphonse, for inviting us over for dinner."

"You're very welcome Lizzy, and you, too, Amy."

"This food looks delicious."

"I'm sure it is. Let's show our gratitude for it. Oh, mighty God, who owns the cattle on a thousand hills and who has materially enriched many among us, we thank you for this food, which many do not have, but who must turn to get help from Dough for the Desperate. Lord, please put your hand on the hearts of Elizabeth and Amelia here, and help them to realize how they need to support this great ministry with generous contributions. We all agree together. Amen. Now, please pass the potatoes."

Of course, it would have been okay *in a private prayer* to ask the Lord to inspire Elizabeth and Amelia to do God's will in regard to donating, but to ask God aloud in their presence to help them "realize" that they should donate is just pure manipulation.

If Fred is praying aloud with and for Sheila, there is a world of difference between, "Lord help Sheila make the decision that pleases you," and "Lord, let Sheila understand that she needs to volunteer to cook for the campout."

A prayer that is perfectly okay to direct to the Lord can become manipulative if prayed aloud when the subject of the prayer is present and likely resistant to the prayer's content. For example, take this prayer: "Dear God, please help Jane and Rebekah to make peace with each other and become friends once again." Prayed alone in your prayer sanctuary or even silently as you sit near the women, these words form a noble and well intentioned request. But prayed aloud in the presence of the women, unless they are both seriously seeking reconciliation, the prayer will almost certainly be interpreted as a psychological ploy, regardless of how sincerely it is made.

Lying to God.

You can lie to Aunt Edna and she will believe you; you can lie to yourself and you might even believe yourself. But you can't lie to God, a being who knows your every thought—and whether those thoughts have any connection to reality. I mean, just what are you thinking?

It is certainly permissible to vent to God. Rant and rave and fume and boil (but please don't curse). Just make sure that in the process you are being honest with God and yourself. In other words, be fair. Angry people who want to yell and complain about all the wrongs that have been visited upon them have a tendency to stack the deck in their favor. Exaggerating, generalizing from one or two instances, leaving out conflicting evidence—who do these people think they are, campaigning politicians?

The point is that you can't use selected instances or slanted arguments with God. Examine your mood and attitude before you go in front of the throne, and make sure you can tell it straight—and with humility and respect.

సం 🕊 ఇ

A PRAYER ADMITTING A HARD HEART

Lord God, I need your help. I want to forgive Edna, but it's hard. Help me Lord. Soften my heart with understanding and enable me truly and completely to forgive her. Forgive me for such hardness that I am finding forgiveness so difficult. And may I always remember from the Lord's Prayer that my own hope for forgiveness depends on my forgiving others. Thank you. In Jesus' name I pray. Amen.

Asking for something that violates Biblical teaching.

When you first opened the box on a new toy you had just purchased, you might have seen a note just inside: "Please read the manual before calling support. Most of the questions you might have are covered there." Similarly, before opening the prayer line to God so that you can ask for something, read the Bible to see if your request harmonizes with the rules.

Prayers that run contrary to Scripture include:

- prayers that serve your pride, greed, lust, hatred, etc.
- prayers asking God to send people to hell
- prayers to win the lottery or otherwise become instantly rich and powerful
- prayers to unmake a problem

✝

📖

Finally, brethren, whatever is true, whatever is honorable, whatever is right, whatever is pure, whatever is lovely, whatever is of good repute, if there is any excellence and if anything worthy of praise, dwell on these things.

—Philippians 4:8 (NASB)

UNANSWERED PRAYER

"Hey Fred. What's going on? You look totally bummed."

"Yeah. It's okay. It's just that God has completely let me down."

"Oh? What happened?"

"He didn't answer my prayer."

"What did you pray for?"

"I asked God to make my wife understand that I need another giant screen TV."

"And God said No?"

"Yeah. I prayed for a week and Tina's still against it."

"Too bad."

"Too bad? It's tragic. What's wrong with God? I mean, the TV I have is over a year old and the new technology is so great and I can get a 70-inch to replace my 60-inch at such a great deal."

"You know, Fred. I feel really sorry for you."

"Thanks, man. But it's God's fault, you know."

✛ ✛ ✛

Chapter 5 Questions for Thought and Discussion

1. Have you ever asked God to do something or give you something that you later understood was

wrong to ask for? What made you realize that? What did you do? What was the ultimate outcome?

2. When we get desperate, we sometimes are tempted to try to bargain with God. Have you ever gotten into that place? Explain the circumstances and the ultimate resolution.

Chapter 5 Activities

1. Think of an urgent situation that could produce a desperate appeal by someone involved. Examples include a family member with cancer, a child in an automobile accident, a parent with Alzheimer's. Write a prayer that avoids bargaining with or attempting to bribe God, but that handles the situation in a heartfelt way.

2. Think about past prayers you have offered. Did you ask for the How as well as the What? Were both answered, one, neither? How did God's How compare with yours?

Chapter 5 Group Activities

1. As a group, brainstorm a list of things that should not be prayed for or that God should not be asked to do. Next to each item, give a reason why the request should be avoided.

2. As a group, examine the list made in #1 above and arrange it in order from least objectionable to most objectionable.

3. Group members should share with the others how the two group activities above have impacted their own prayer life.

6

God's Role in Prayer

To pray well to God, you need only an ardent heart.
— Proverb

Before you pray, it's important to know to whom you are praying. We sometimes forget that we are addressing the creator of the universe, the being who created us, cares about us and already knows our wants and needs — and what's good or bad for us — before we ever open our hearts to him.

This is obvious, you say. But judging by the way many people talk about their relationship with God and their expectations for him, there seems to be a lot of confusion over the relationship between God and the person praying, and the purpose of prayer itself. For example, prayers of request are just that — requests. They are not demands. Our role in prayer is to worship, thank, praise, and celebrate God, and also humbly to bring our needs before him, to request his help.

If there is any lingering doubt about who God is and what you should expect when you pray, here are a few comments about who God is NOT, in the hope that they will help clarify who he is.

God is not your butler.

Listen to some people pray and it's always about themselves and their needs:

"God, bring me this."

"God, I need this."

"Lord, come on, I want this."

You've heard this kind of thing. "James, bring me the newspaper." Compare that to, "God, bring me a wife."

A major component of prayer is to present God with your requests, but it must be done with a right heart and humble attitude. God is not your butler. If the only prayers you pray are the gimme prayers—

God gimme money, God gimme a house,
God gimme a better job, God gimme a spouse.

—then you've got the relationship backwards. You are to be his servant, not vice versa. Yes, we are to pray for our needs and for others—see Matthew 6 and 7. But remember that God will sometimes be saying No to you.

In the worst cases of "God is my butler," some people will pray for something with almost an entitlement attitude, and when they don't get it, they become indignant and declare that they are "through with God." See? God is your butler, or maybe just a delivery boy, and when he doesn't show up with your exact order—and pretty quick, too—you scold him and then fire him. But is that really your view of God and his purpose in the universe and your role on earth? Just think what the world would be like if God immediately granted every prayer request.

ಬಂ 🕊 ಄
A PRAYER ABOUT GOD'S SOVEREIGNTY

I realize, O Lord, that I sometimes ask for a lot, for myself especially. And sometimes I half expect you to say yes and give me what I want. In such times, dear Father, remind me that I'm your servant and not the other way around. Remind me, too, that you know what's best for me and for others and for your kingdom, and that my understanding is limited.

So, in spite of how urgently or expectantly I pray, do your perfect will in the answer and help me to trust you in the outcome—especially when the answer is not the one I want. Thank you for putting up with me and loving me in spite of myself. In Jesus' name. Amen.

God is not a vending machine.

Some people think that when you want something, you pray. The bigger the thing you want, the more prayers you need to put in. One prayer might get you a cold drink on a hot day, but you'll need lots of prayers to get a new car. Big cost, big prayers. Put in a prayer, get what you want.

If this isn't how prayer works, what's the point?

But what does Jesus say about this vending machine view of God?

✝
📖

And when you pray, do not heap up empty phrases as the Gentiles do, for they think that they will be heard for their many words. Do not be like them, for your Father knows what you need before you ask him.

—Matthew 6:7-8 (ESV)

Just as bad, if not worse, is the actual cash vending machine delusion. Need something? Like saving your soul? Put in a tithe, buy your way to heaven. You don't even have to push the selection button.

And whether you put in prayers or cash, if God doesn't deliver, you kick that machine and walk away. You stop putting in your coins. Done with that God. Changing from Coke to Pepsi. But just what does such behavior reveal? It shows that you never actually loved God, never had a real relationship with him. You had a transactional relationship, and you were in it for what you could get out of it.

You see, real Christians serve God for who he is, not for the soda he can dispense when they drop in a coin. Have you ever had a human relationship where the other person "liked" you only for what you could deliver? And when you could or would no longer deliver, the relationship was over? Think how God must feel about people who view him like this.

Your Treasure in Heaven

"Hey, Reece, why are you slamming that ball against the wall? Let's do some one-on-one."

"Forget it, Big Man. I'm stewing."

"Over what? Natasha treating you like you deserve again?"

"No, man. It's God. He's not coming through."

"Example me, bud."

"I pray and try to be good and even go to church at Christmas, but I still live in a two-bedroom apartment with my parents, my sister, and my little brother."

"And? So?"

"Well, look how God blessed Solomon."

"And you think you should be blessed likewise?"

"Well, at least a nice four-bedroom house in the suburbs, a really sharp wife, and a new car."

"And what about your family?"

"They can pray for their own stuff. If I got mine, I'd be outta here."

"What do you think God gave to the couple who took the responsibility to birth and raise the Son of God?"

"I don't know. What?"

"Other than little gold and some spices at Jesus' birth, God didn't give Mary and Joseph anything special. No villa or independent wealth or anything. In fact, Joseph had to work all his life as a carpenter and stone mason, laboring to feed about ten children. He died before the crucifixion, leaving Mary a widow."

"Really?"

"And then they had the worry about Jesus, as he traveled around teaching and getting into trouble with the authorities. Finally, Mary witnessed her son being tortured and murdered in a very cruel way."

"And they still loved God?"

"Very much. They knew their service would be rewarded in heaven. They loved God and were grateful to have had the opportunity to serve him with their whole lives."

"I don't know what to say."

"Good."

ဆဝ 🕊 ର

A PRAYER ABOUT UNMERITED GRACE

Lord, I realize that I can't buy your answer to my prayers with money. And I also know that and I can't gain your favor merely by offering a huge number of prayers. Then, too, I realize that you know what I need before I ask. So please, Lord, help me to remember that you are my God and that any blessing you give to me comes not from my merit but through your grace. May my prayers, many or few, be offered by me and received by you with the knowledge of your sovereignty and of your merciful consideration. Thank you. In Jesus' name. Amen.

God is not an insurance policy.

It's rather scary to hear people say, "I don't have any fire insurance because I believe God won't let my house burn down." These people seem to think that believing in God prevents all harm. Once we graciously deign to believe in God, the least he can do for us is provide us with insurance and prevent any misfortune from befalling us.

And then, of course, your spouse divorces you or your house does burn down. And what is the result? Yep. It's another one of those "done with God" farces: "I trusted God. He let me down, so now I'm through with him."

What does Jesus tell us?

✝
📖

In the world you will have tribulation. But take heart; I have overcome the world.
—John 16:33b (ESV)

I don't see anywhere (and I've read the Bible several times) that Jesus says, "If you believe in me I won't let your house burn down."

When you believe in God on the wrong terms, you are bound to be disappointed with his unfathomable ways. If you expect God to guarantee, say, your job, and you are fired just before Christmas, God seems to you to be an inept insurance company.

On the other hand, if you realize that God's job is not to organize his day to make sure that nothing bad ever happens to you, and if you recognize him as the one who knows what is best for the entire creation—in spite of the workings of the Evil One—then you won't be surprised when suffering comes.

Study the lives and deaths of the apostles. Not a pretty ending for many of them. Crucified, burned, tortured, body parts cut off—they didn't act outraged at God because he let these things happen.

By the way, some people like to say that they are "trusting God" to heal them or get a job or bring them a spouse, and so on. What this really means is that they are expecting God to do their will instead of his will. And if he doesn't do what they want, that will mean that he is breaking their trust and that such a betrayal justifies their leaving him.

Trust God to be God and to love you—through good and bad. Trust God to do his executive will, which will be for the best for humanity. Trust God to redeem even the worst of events. But don't make statements that amount to vague threats, saying that you are trusting God to do what you want.

✝
📖

For as the heavens are higher than the earth, so are my ways higher than your ways and my thoughts than your thoughts.

—Isaiah 55:9 (ESV)

৪৩ 🕊 ৫৪

A PRAYER OF ASSURANCE

Dear God, I understand that in this life, we will all experience many trials and pains and that there are no guarantees of health or safety. That's why we are always so grateful when you answer our prayers for protection and safe journeys and recovery from illnesses. When it is not your will to spare us from some event of sorrow or suffering, I pray that you will enable us to face it with endurance and courage and trust in you. And I ask that you'll reassure us of our heavenly home, where your eternal kingdom has forever banished pain, grief, and tears. In the name of the Lord Jesus. Amen.

God is not a school boy.

Some people love God so much that they want to raise him up in the right way by teaching him what to do and how to behave.

How else can we understand prayers like these:

"God, don't you know how much I need this new cell phone?"

"God, don't you understand how much I need Jane?"

"God, I absolutely must score at least in the 95th percentile on this exam. If I don't, I won't get into the grad school I need to for my planned career. So you can see how important this is, and why you've got to help me."

And when the schoolboy God doesn't do the right thing, he gets chastised: "God, why aren't you acting here? I need your power right now."

It must be very gratifying to these people to realize that when they make these kinds of statements and ask these kinds of questions, they are implying that they know something God doesn't know. Must be a real ego boost to be able to lecture God.

†
📖

For, "Who can know the LORD's thoughts? Who knows enough to teach Him?"
—1 Corinthians 2:16a (NLT)

☙ 🕊 ❧
A PRAYER TO LEARN FROM GOD

Dear Lord, forgive me for getting upset and seeming to lecture you. My anxiety and fear have pushed me into this foolishness. Please do your good and perfect will with this issue, and just ignore me when I get out of line. I trust you. You know everything, and I don't. I'm like a little bug trying to tell the rain where to fall in a huge forest.

Teach me your ways, O Lord, and let me learn your heart. Help me to discern your will and to love it and to follow it with joy. Thank you for being so understanding and merciful. In Jesus' name. Amen.

God is not your debtor.

We are in debt to God for giving us our being, for providing us with many blessings, and for buying us out of the punishment we deserve for sin. But how do some people act?

THE DEBTOR

"Hi, Jane. Why the angry look?"

"Mr. Simpkins just gave Harvey the promotion he was supposed to give to me."

"Oh, I'm sorry. Do you think it had something to do with the Dinktronics contract?

"That wasn't my fault. And this whole failure to get the promotion isn't my fault, either."

"No?"

"No, it isn't. It's God's fault. And I'm mad at him."

"Uh, God's fault? What did he ever do to you?"

"That's just the point. I gave a big donation to a charity, and I let God know what is was for. But Harvey gets my promotion."

"Well, I'm not sure—."

"I mean, I'm entitled to that promotion. Why didn't God pay up?"

"I think you're—."

"He owes me."

It is often said that we are an entitlement society, where everyone thinks everyone else owes them everything. Students think they are entitled to an A in class just because they showed up much of the time. Workers think they should be rated "Exceeds Expectations" just because they came to work most days and did only what they were told to do.

But we have no entitlement with God. He doesn't owe us anything. On the contrary, we owe him not only our very existence but our salvation, together with an uncountable number of undeserved blessings.

ɞ 🕊 ҩ

A PRAYER OF GRATITUDE

Dear God, I pause to come to you in joy at the wonderful blessings you pour out on me every day. You give me an abundance of food, a comfortable place to live, and meaningful work to do. More than these, I bless you for my five senses. I can smell the aromas of cooking and the freshness of clean towels; I can taste the food set before me and the crispness of cold water; I can hear the speech of others and listen to the music I love; I can see the beauty of the natural world and look into the eyes of my loved ones; I can touch the rough bark of a tree and the smooth handshake of a friend. Your blessings are infinite. How could I ever name them all? For these I have named and all the others, I am deeply grateful, Lord. In the name of Jesus, I thank you. Amen.

✝
📖

Who has given to Me that I should repay him? Whatever is under the whole heaven is Mine.
—Job 41:11a (NASB)

God is not your debate opponent.

Some people think that prayer can be used to convince God that he's wrong and that they have the better arguments and reasons.

But when God says,

✝
📖

Come now, and let us reason together.
—Isaiah 1:18 (NASB)

he doesn't mean that you should attempt to out argue him. He means that you should listen to reason. And God has all the arguments.

Approach God with humility and reverence, knowing that he is already aware of your thoughts, feelings, needs, wants — and reasons.

✝

📖

Don't worry about anything; instead, pray about everything. Tell God what you need, and thank Him for all He has done.

—Philippians 4:6 (NLT)

౭ 🕊 ౬

A PRAYER TO ACCEPT GOD'S WAYS

Dear Lord, I pray that you will enable me to accept your will and your ways with my life and that I won't try to second guess what you ordain. Help me to know what your plans are for me and to work for their success. And let me know where you want me to make my own choices. Give me the wisdom I need to make them well. Thank you for understanding my sometimes questioning heart, and forgive me. May your will be done in all things, always. In Jesus' name. Amen.

God is not a yes man.

Yes, indeed, God answers every prayer. But the answer is not always Yes. In fact, there are many answers other than Yes. And all of them with the righteousness of his kingdom and our personal good in mind. See Chapter 9: How Does God Answer Prayer?

Expecting God to be a Yes man and agree with every prayer you offer would imply that you are of unfailingly accurate discernment, perfect understanding, and faultless decision making. But you're not. Nor are you fully objective, completely impartial, and always just. Your humanness at least occasionally interferes with your thinking process. (Sorry if I'm the first person to inform you of this.)

॰ 🕊 ॰

A PRAYER TO HONOR GOD'S WISDOM

My dear God, thank you so much for being the source and sum of all wisdom, and for guiding us in it. Continue to open my eyes to your truth, that I might gain insight and understanding into my own nature and the nature of other people. Give me from your wisdom the wisdom I need to make good choices and to help others to do the same. I bless your name for granting me such knowledge and for being "the only wise God." In Jesus' name. Amen.

✝

📖

"For My thoughts are not your thoughts, Nor are your ways My ways," declares the LORD. "For as the heavens are higher than the earth, So are My ways higher than your ways And My thoughts than your thoughts."

—Isaiah 55:8-9 (NASB)

God is not a Formula-One pit crew.

The last time you prayed for something, how long did you expect to wait before the answer came? Ten years? Okay, five? No? A few months or weeks, then. No? You expected it immediately—or if you are a monument to patience, the day after tomorrow.

The expectation of a Yes answer, delivered in an hour, smacks of butlerism again. Just because our culture promotes the desire for instant gratification, we shouldn't think that God ought to be in a similar hurry to indulge us.

✝
📖

For in Your sight a thousand years are like yesterday
that passes by, like a few hours of the night.
— Psalm 90:4 (HCSB)

The harsh truth is, more often than not, God is not in a
hurry. He knows that if we take the time and make the
effort to think things through, we will likely change
our request at least somewhat, because in our haste to
bring the problem to God, we often misunderstand the
situation and therefore ask for the wrong things.
Thankfully, God is patient with us. And remember that
his great plan stretches from one end of eternity to the
other, down the stairs and up the ladder, across the
street and behind the barn.

✝
📖

Rejoice in hope, be patient in tribulation, be constant
in prayer.
— Romans 12:12 (ESV)

Not to be too boringly autobiographical, I once prayed
for something and was answered within seconds. Another time my prayers were answered only after 19
years. In both cases, God's timing was best.

🕊
A PRAYER FOR PATIENCE

Dear Lord, I realize that I have become a product of
my instant-gratification culture, a culture that has
trained me to want everything immediately. But I
also realize that you deal with me on your own
schedule, and that I must be patient in everything.
So I ask you now, please help me to become a trust-

ing child who waits on your will with hope and faith, knowing that your timing is best. Help me not to expect every prayer to be answered immediately, but to know that your plans for my welfare and the good of the world involve waiting — without complaint. Thank you for this gift. In Jesus' name. Amen.

God is not your abusive father.

It seems that many people get their idea of God from their fathers. A kind, loving father gives them belief in a kind, loving God. A stern, rejecting father results in a God who has little love for them. Many of the angry atheist writers had abusive, absent, or rejecting fathers.

But your view of God should come from the Bible and from your personal relationship with his loving son, Jesus.

ℬ 🕊 ℛ

A PRAYER TO SEE GOD AS HE IS

Dear Lord, I come to you as the child of an abusive father. He treated me badly, and I now realize that my view of you has been corrupted by my feelings about him. I must admit that I have seen you as a cold, unloving, even punishing God because that was my earthly father. But your word tells me and shows me that you are a kind, loving, merciful God, who came to earth in human form in order to show us what it is like to love.

I need your help to replace my distorted ideas — and more, my poisoned feelings — with the true knowledge and genuine feelings that I am loved and cared for by you. Give me the welcoming heart that you deserve. May I now and forever see you as you are, and not as something influenced by earthly sorrow. In Jesus' name I praise you and thank you. Amen.

God is not your cleaning lady.

Too many people turn to God only when they have messed up hugely and want him to deliver them from the consequences of their actions. As more than one wit has noted, these people are asking God to make two and two not equal to four.

"Dear God, I've been arrested for drug possession. Help me get out of this without any problem."

God's purpose in the cosmos is not to clean up after you create a mess, either for yourself or for others.

That said, God often does help those who cause their own disasters. If he didn't, none of us would get much divine aid. Sometimes, however, the answer to prayer differs from what we ask. Instead of removing the mountain in front of us, he helps us to climb the mountain.

ℬ 🕊 ℭ

A PRAYER TO TAKE RESPONSIBILITY

Lord, I'm in big trouble and I know it's all my own fault. I don't deserve your attention, much less your help, but I turn to you, seeking your mercy. I deeply repent of the actions that have left me in this situation. I am so sorry for the trouble I have caused others and the disgust I have caused you by my disobedience to your commandments. If it pleases you, please help me through this trouble. Be my guide and work in the hearts of those I have harmed and those in whose power I now am. May they show mercy also. Whatever comes, dear God, know that my repentance is real and that I will do whatever is necessary to improve my life and my Christian walk. Thank you for not giving up on me, but for loving me in spite of my sins. Help me for Jesus' sake. Amen.

✠✠✠

Chapter 6 Questions for Thought and Discussion

1. Which, if any, of the improper views of God have you ever had when you prayed for something? What caused this attitude? How did you overcome it?

2. What would you say to someone who "gave up on God" because of an unanswered prayer?

3. What would you say to someone who believes that God owes them something?

Chapter 6 Activities

1. Draw a line down the center of a piece of paper, making two columns. In the left column, write down ten characteristics and behaviors of your earthly father. Was or is he kind, generous, understanding? Was or is he selfish, mean, abusive? Warm or cold toward you? Lax or a disciplinarian?

    Next, in the right column, write down ten characteristics of God, taken from the Bible. (See, for example, Deuteronomy 4:31, 2 Chronicles 30:9b, Psalm 59:9, Psalm 62:8 and Psalm 73:28.)

    Finally, compare the lists. Does your father seem to be a Godly man? If your earthly father has some negative characteristics, keep this list to remind you of the differences between your earthly and heavenly fathers.

2. Choose three of the wrong views of God and write a contrary view that shows a genuine view of God.

Chapter 6 Group Activities

1. Discuss with the group what makes an ideal parent? Agree on ten positive characteristics (those that are most desirable in a parent) and ten negative characteristics (those least desirable in a parent). Discuss why each characteristic was put on each list.
2. Have the group make a list of characteristics that apply to God, listed as "God is —." such as "God is generous." Stop at a reasonable number (10, 25, etc.) and discuss them.

7

Preparing to Pray

> *After I enter the chapel, I place myself in the presence of God and I say to him, "Lord here I am; give me whatever you wish." Then I begin to tell him of all that concerns me, my joys, my thoughts, my distress, and finally, I listen to him.*
>
> — *Catherine Laboure*

In an environment filled with busyness, distractions, temptations, the fear of "missing something," interruptions, worries, and to-do lists, how do you ever find the time to pray? More importantly, how can you clear your mind and focus on talking to God? To respond to this challenge, let's look at some ideas for improving your prayer experience.

Choose an appropriate time and place.

Try to choose the same time each day for your Bible reading, worship, and prayers. Ideally, choose the first thing in the morning for your scheduled time with God. Make a cup of tea or coffee or pour some juice, and open your heart and mind, open the Word, and open your talk with God. As I said, we live in a distracted world, and unless you commit decidedly to a specific time and place—and protect it fiercely—chances are you'll get busy and never get around to charging up your spiritual batteries.

PRIORITIES

[cell phone rings]

"Hello? Norma?"

"Hi, Jan. What's news?"

"My big news is that I can't talk now, because I've got a new life plan."

"What's it all about?"

"The very first thing I'm going to do every day is read the Bible and pray."

"That sounds great. I was just calling to see if you wanted to go to breakfast first. The Saturday breakfast special at Stuffums, that includes pie, is over in twenty minutes. If we go right now, we can just make it."

"Well, I—."

"And you'll be able to concentrate better on the Word if your stomach isn't growling."

"That's true, I guess."

"I'll be outside your door in three minutes."

"Well, okay."

. . . .

"Thanks for this idea, Norma. It was great to have breakfast with you. And that news about Sam and Gina. I can't believe half of it."

"Oh, Jan! Look at this ad! Frimpkins department store is having a two-hour sale, on today, with discounts of 50 to 70 percent off! It's over at noon, and it's just ten minutes after eleven now. We can still make it, if we hurry. I know a shortcut."

"But my Bible reading and prayer time—."

"You can do that first thing after we see what the bargains are."

. . . .

"Thanks for driving, Norma. We got some really good stuff."

"You bet we did."

"See you later."

"Bye."

[cell phone rings]

"Hello?"

"Hey Jan."

"Oh Hi Judy."

"What's up?"

"Not much. I was just getting ready to have my prayer and Bible reading time."

"That's great. Say, did you hear about Sam and Gina?"

"Only a snippet. What did you hear?"

. . . .

"I can't believe all that can be true, Judy. Are you sure?"

"Absolutely. Say, Jan, I've got to take the dog to the vet at four, so I'd better let you go."

"Four? Yikes! Look at the time. It's 3:30 and I still haven't done my Bible reading."

"Well, I'll let you get to it."

"Ok, thanks. But really, I'm feeling so sleepy, and I won't be able to concentrate. So I'll take a short nap first. Bye Judy."

"Bye, Jan."

. . . .

[phone rings]

"Huh? Hello? What?"

"Hey, Sweetheart. Did I wake you?"

"Fred? No, no, I was just resting a bit."

"You haven't forgotten that we're going out for dinner tonight and then to the new Marvin Stunman movie, *Attack of the Time Zombies*?"

"Oh, that's right. Okay, okay."

"I'll be home in about twenty minutes. Are you dressed yet?"

"Twenty minutes? Aren't you still watching the game with Chou?"

"It's over."

"What time is—oh, no, it's quarter to six already!"

"Right. See you soon my love. Bye."

. . . .

"Well, Sweetheart, how did you like the movie?"

"Too many exploding helicopters and too many flesh-eating dead people."

"But those were the best parts."

"I'm exhausted. It'll be midnight by the time we get home and I have an early day tomorrow."

"Oh? What are you going to do?"

"I've got a new plan. The very first thing I'm going to do every day is read the Bible and pray."

"Great, Sweetheart. It's great to make the Lord a priority in your life."

Clear your mind.

This advice comes from cognitive theory. Your brain can handle at one time only so much—and that's not much—information in present, conscious memory. If you have things to do and haven't written them down, they can hog your working memory. You'll recognize this if you've ever had a prayer like this:

ℰ𝒪 🕊 ℭ𝒬

A PRAYER ABOUT ???

Dear Lord, thank you for blessing me with the new shirt [uh oh, I forgot to pick up the laundry at the cleaners and they close at 5 and it's already 4]—I mean, thank you for all the blessings you pour out [and we're out of milk, and I'd better check the bread] — sorry, Lord, I appreciate all you do for me and my family [that's right; I haven't changed Jenny's Band-Aid today] — um, well, dear Lord [*reiterate* – that was the word I was trying to think of earlier]. Sorry, Lord. Amen.

When I worked designing instructional materials, I created a sheet for students to use for taking notes. Power Notes, as they were called, included a small area called the sandbox, where students could write down whatever was on their minds, such as buying onions or calling Fred, thus freeing up their working memory for learning. That is, they didn't need to keep repeating their to-do or "worry about" items over and over in their minds as a way of remembering them. They simply wrote them down.

As a helpful way of clearing your mind, then, write down everything that is occupying your mind — errands, actions, chores, tasks, ideas, movie scripts, whatever it might be. Turn the paper over or put it in the back of your Bible so that it's out of sight.

†

📖

Be earnest and disciplined in your prayers.
— 1 Peter 4:7b (NLT)

Find a quiet physical environment.

Find a quiet place where you can be safely alone, uninterrupted. The place should not have distractions. This means

- Avoid places with windows with views of the busy world (such as a highway).

- Turn off the TV, radio, music player, PC screen.
- Turn off your cell phone or leave it in another room, set to silent. This might be the most important piece of advice since many of us have become addicted to phone messages, and whether it rings to announce a call, buzzes to announce a text message, dings to announce an incoming email, or calls attention to itself to announce a Twitter or other message, we are immediately distracted and have to see what this "important" message is all about. So, temporarily say, "Away with this attention thief."
- Clear the desk or table of everything other than a Bible and your prayer journal and a pen.

Read some Scripture.

Reading from God's word is an excellent way of bringing your mind into a prayerful mood. In the Old Testament, reading from the book of Psalms can be rewarding because many of the Psalms are poem-prayers, covering a range of thought and feelings. There is joy and sorrow, hope and fear, request and thanksgiving.

Before you read, always ask for help from the Lord to give you understanding and insight. Remember that every time you read a passage, it will resonate with you differently. That's the Spirit's work.

ഌ 🕊 ∝
A PRAYER BEFORE READING THE BIBLE

Dear God, you are the author of all truth, all knowledge, and all wisdom. And you have given these things to us in your word. As I read, I ask that your Holy Spirit will illuminate my mind and heart, giving me understanding of your word, that I might gain a better knowledge of you and your will for my life. Teach me your truth, for your word is truth. In Jesus' name I thank you. Amen.

Examine your motives.

If, as is common, you are going to ask for God's help or action in some situation, first ask yourself why. Why are you going to ask for the things you are going to ask for? Normally, this question can be answered quickly and simply because normally your motives and intentions are pure. You're in a right relationship with God and your requests are unselfish and reflect a kind intention.

But if, for some reason, you are feeling angry or selfish or even hateful, stop and examine your heart and what you are thinking of asking God to do for you.

✝
📖
Yet even when you do pray, your prayers are not answered, because you pray just for selfish reasons.
— James 4:3 (NASB)

If necessary, go back and reread Chapter 5 about why some prayers go unanswered.

✝
📖
We may think we know what is right, but the LORD is the judge of our motives.
— Proverbs 16:12 (CEV)

Establish yourself in the presence of God.

Once you are quiet and undisturbed, come deliberately, intentionally, and feelingly into God's presence by concentrating on him. Focus your thoughts and pray.

ૹ 🕊 ஐ

A PRAYER FOR ENTERING GOD'S PRESENCE

Dear God, I know that you are always with me and that I am therefore always in your presence. But I want to feel that you are with me now and establish myself consciously in your presence. Please be with me as I talk with you, communicating spirit to Spirit. And help me to draw ever closer to you. Thank you so very much. I ask for Jesus' sake. Amen.

Now you should be ready to open your prayer journal and begin to pray for those people and circumstances on your list and in your heart.

✢✢✢

Chapter 7 Questions for Thought and Discussion

1. What is your habitual method for entering God's presence to worship him and ask for your needs?
2. How would you counsel someone who has never felt God's presence?
3. Chapter 1 said that, in following Jesus' declaration about the greatest commandment, prayer should involve heart, soul, mind, and strength. If that is so, does being in God's presence require feeling it? Or can you know you are in God's presence by your worship, prayer, and Scripture reading? Can the

emotion or feeling come as a result of prayer rather than a precursor to prayer?

4. Do you ever do a "motive" check before you pray? Have you ever found that you were about to ask for something with a less than good motive?

Chapter 7 Activities

1. Take this chapter's advice about setting up a safe, quiet place where you can pray and read the Bible uninterruptedly. After a week of daily practice, think about whether the setup suits you. What do you like about it? What do you not like about it? What do you want to change? Will you continue to use this space?

2. In your prayer journal, make notes of your prayers for a few days or a week. Read them over and analyze them for your attitude toward God and for your motives. Do you have a humble attitude and unselfish motives? Or are there some areas that need work?

3. Write out some of your prayers in advance so that you can capture exactly what you want to pray about. Pray these prayers and compare them with your unwritten ones.

Chapter 7 Group Activities

1. Members of the group should each share their favorite setting for Bible reading and prayer. Is there a special place? room? chair? table? What kinds of resources are placed nearby? dictionary? commentary? Bible dictionary? other aids?

2. Group members should share their individual ways of entering into God's presence. Are there similarities among the methods shared?

3. As a group, brainstorm possible methods of entering into God's presence while away from a convenient location: (1) on a train or airplane, (2) at a convention or conference, (3) in a stadium or arena. Remember to look for an effective method, not a wooden formula.

8

How Should We Pray?

> *There are moments when, whatever be the attitude of the body, the soul is on its knees.*
> — *Victor Hugo*

Social arrangements.

There are many possibilities for praying either by yourself or with others.

Pray by Yourself, Silently. Many praying people do a substantial amount of their praying alone with God. By praying silently, they can be genuine and not feel the need to hold anything back. No self-censorship, euphemizing, omitting, or otherwise sanitizing their faults. Another advantage to praying silently is that you can do it anywhere — in a crowded elevator, a business meeting, a classroom, an airport.

Pray by Yourself, Aloud. Often, people find that praying aloud helps them stay focused on God and the prayer. They feel that their prayers become more real and their relationship with God more personal. They also listen to what they are saying, which allows for some introspection and self-knowledge.

Pray with a Prayer Partner. It can be very helpful to find someone who can come alongside you in agreement and to pray for the pressing needs of yourself or others—healing, salvation, guidance. It is also a joyful experience to worship, praise, and thank God for answered prayer or for the wonderful life he has given you. Spouses make an ideal prayer partner because praying together allows them to share their spiritual and worldly concerns. And just as prayer helps to develop a relationship with God, shared prayer helps to develop the relationship between the spouses.

Pray Privately. In the old days, many people had a "prayer closet," which was a small, private room to which they could retreat to focus their thoughts, read the Bible, and pray. For busy, distracted people, setting aside a personal space like this can provide a refuge, an escape from the too many tasks to do and permit some thought gathering. Most modern homes don't have dedicated prayer spaces, but if you look around your own home or apartment, there might be a space you can use in the garage, laundry room, spare bedroom, and so forth. Some homes have walk-in closets big enough for a chair and small desk.

Pray Publicly. Praying in public, such as saying grace in a restaurant, praying for a safe flight on an airliner, or praying for inspiration in a Sunday School class, has several benefits. It demonstrates to the unsaved that you are a child of God. It reminds them that some people recognize God as the sovereign master of the universe and of humans. It models, for young and old, good Christian behavior. It encourages you and others to be bold in the faith. And it spreads Christian faith to all those who hear what you say. Public prayers can be offered by you, with just one other person, or with a large group.

The only caution here is that some people think they must pray in an artificial, oratorical, almost bombastic style to make their prayer sound impressive to the others around them who hear it. Remember the advice above, however, and pray in your "ordinary" style. This is best both because God is your primary audience and because those who hear and pray with you will feel the sincerity and genuineness of the communication.

If you are used to praying aloud by yourself, especially in public, you might have adopted a soft, quiet tone. That's fine. But when you pray aloud with another person or a small group, be sure to enunciate clearly and to use an adequate volume. A soft, quiet prayer to an audience will likely not be heard or understood.

THE RETREAT

"Hey Tom. How was the retreat?"

"Great. Great."

"What was it like?"

"We had these great talks about growing in faith and becoming better people."

"Oh, it was a religious retreat?

"Yeah, yeah. At the end of every talk Pastor Smith bowed his head and mumbled something for a couple of minutes. Once I think I heard him say the word *Lord*. I think he might have been praying."

What should be your posture?

Over many lands in many ages, people have adopted different physical positions when they pray.

The best position for you is the one that causes you to feel you're in God's presence. Different positions at different times might be suitable.

Kneeling. Praying on your knees is a time-honored posture. It can be done in front of the living room sofa, by the bedside, or other place. A kneeling position and a bowed head reminds you of God's exalted position and your humble dependence on him.

✝

📖

Therefore humble yourselves under the mighty hand of God, that He may exalt you at the proper time, casting all your anxiety on Him, because He cares for you.

—1 Peter 5:6-7 (NASB)

Lying Face Down. In past ages, some people showed their submission to God by lying face down and extending their arms, forming a cross with their bodies. This position reflects complete resignation and often deep repentance.

Standing. Remember when gentlemen stood up out of respect whenever a lady entered the room? Or, perhaps your church asks the congregation to stand when God's word is read. Standing in these cases is a sign of honor and respect. It follows, then, that standing for prayer is a good choice. Standing seems to give different thought processes than does sitting or lying down.

Sitting. Sitting is a practical position. If you pray while you drive, it's the only option. Similarly, if you read Scripture or other devotional material while you pray at intervals, sitting, such as sitting at a desk or the kitchen table, is practical.

Lying on Your Back. Those who pray their final prayer of the day often do so either kneeling at the bedside or in bed ready for sleep. Lying down this way is usually a less optimal position for general prayer times, because it tends to tell the brain to lose focus and go to sleep. But for those who are bedridden or hospitalized, it's the position of necessity.

Walking. Many people discover that taking a leisurely stroll through a park, along a beach, or on a trail in the woods offers an ideal time to collect their thoughts, settle their spirit, and pray. Even a walk around the block in the neighborhood can work.

Floating. Yes, even floating on an inner tube or other device can provide the quiet, alone time that encourages prayer. The point is, find a position that feels the most comfortable and reverential, and use that.

How long should your personal prayers be?

As you will no doubt recall, Jesus warns his disciples not to make their prayers intentionally long just so they will be heard:

✝

📖

And when you are praying, do not use meaningless repetition as the Gentiles do, for they suppose that they will be heard for their many words. So do not be like them; for your Father knows what you need before you ask Him.
— Matthew 6:7-8 (NASB)

My interpretation of Jesus' teaching is this: It's okay to pray for something every day or six times a day, if you keep your prayer short and to the point.

What Jesus teaches is that we shouldn't elaborate our prayers with needless wordage. Compare these prayers:

ഇ 🕊 ര

A PRAYER FOR HELP WITH A CAR

Dear Lord, please help me sell my old car, so that I can make the down payment on the new one. All according to your will. In Jesus' name. Amen.

ഇ 🕊 ര

ANOTHER PRAYER FOR HELP WITH A CAR

O God, please, please help me get my old car sold and soon. I need that money for a down payment on the new car, and the exact car I want might be sold if you delay. You know how much I need that new car and how broken down the old car is. O Lord, act soon, I pray, and help me get that old clunker off my hands and the cash into my pocket. I need reliable transportation. My job depends on it, and I have three kids to support and they will go hungry if I don't get the new, reliable car. You know I almost got fired once when my car broke down on. . . . etc.

I know, I know. When you are faced with a very emotional and urgent situation, it's tempting to extend your prayer, adding more and more words, even repeating yourself over and over as your anxiety takes control. In such cases, I think the Lord will understand if you do that. Just remember that God already knows what we need, and such elaborations are not necessary. God wants us to pray to show him and ourselves what we really want. A short prayer suffices. Under appropriate circumstances, a long, agonizing prayer surely must be acceptable to our understanding and loving

Lord, but under ordinary circumstances, turning a request into a whine probably doesn't help.

PRAY WITHOUT CEASING

"Hey, Ernie. What are you doing here? You were sitting there this morning when I left. You haven't been here all day, have you?"

"Well, Jewel, that would be a Yes."

"What, exactly, are you doing? You're sitting in the dim light — don't tell me you're trying to study in this light?"

"No, I'm praying. Have been since this morning."

"Praying for twelve, no, thirteen hours?"

"That's right. So now, please excuse me and be quiet. Oh, Lord, Lord, Lord, please help me to pass the licensing exam. I need your blessing to pass this. Help me, help me, help me. Give me the answers, show me which choice to pick, reveal the correct answer to me in every case. Show me how to pick the right answers so I can score very high on the exam and pass with glory and get the license. Guide my pencil, O Lord, to fill in the right bubbles all the way through . . . [et cetera]."

And remember, too, that prayer length is partly a phenomenon of individual personalities: Some people use many more words to convey the same thought than others do. Don't worry about it. Just be yourself in the presence of God. And as Jesus says, don't make your prayers lengthy just to get noticed.

For example, prayers can be very brief when connected to everyday, ordinary tasks, either before you begin or while you work. Such prayers are called emergent prayers because they emerge from a specific

situation. (See Chapter 10.) Here are some of the emergent prayers I've made:

ଛୋ 🕊 ଓଃ

Lord, please help me to fix this door so it won't stick
anymore.

ଛୋ 🕊 ଓଃ

Lord, please help me get this screw started and the
outlet installed correctly—and working! In Jesus'
name. Thanks.

ଛୋ 🕊 ଓଃ

Lord, please send your Spirit to inspire me and illuminate my mind as I work on this prayer book.
And may it glorify and honor you. Thank you in Jesus' name. Amen.

ଛୋ 🕊 ଓଃ

Dear Lord, please help me to have a great meeting
with Joe today. May all that I say be a blessing to
him and an honor to you. And may your Spirit give
me the words to speak. In Jesus' name. Amen.

ଛୋ 🕊 ଓଃ

Lord, we pray that you'll give us a safe trip out to
dinner and a safe trip home. Thank you in your
name. Amen.

ଛୋ 🕊 ଓଃ

Lord, please help me to get well. I feel terrible. For
Jesus' sake. Amen.

ଛୋ 🕊 ଓଃ

Thanks, Lord, for such a great parking space. Yay,
God.

ဢ 🕊 ℃
Dear Lord, please don't let the cake fall!

Okay, I've never prayed that last one. But you get the idea. I try to keep close to God all day, so I talk to him for help, praise, and gratitude frequently and briefly. Just as there is a very short Bible verse, "Jesus wept" (John 11:35), so there can be very short prayers. If you get a sudden flat on the freeway, "Help, Lord" is all the prayer you need as you wrestle the car to a stop.

In these short prayers, you might say I'm "practicing the presence of God" and following Brother Lawrence's advice:

> That we ought to act very simply towards God, speaking frankly to Him, and asking His help in things as they occurred. . . .
> — Second Conversation

How long should a prayer session last?

How much time to devote to personal, extended prayer is an individual decision that varies widely among different people and with the same person on different days. Some people need an hour or two hours of prayer to get fully caught up with God, while others complete their praises and requests in 15 to 30 minutes. Some people like to pray once a day to cover their entire list of needs and thanksgivings, while others pray several times a day.

The best advice to follow is, Make your prayers whatever length they need to be, no longer or shorter. When you have a lot to discuss, you'll have a longer prayer than if you have only one brief thanksgiving or one quick request.

Those who pray several times a day sometimes divide their prayers into themes. A simple example:

- Morning: Thanksgiving and Praise
- Noon: Personal Needs
- Evening: Praying for Others
- Night: World Issues, Government

Whether your communication is long or short, always keep close to your Savior. If you find that praying is difficult for you, feel free to pray for your prayers, too, asking that you will grow more comfortable and easy when you talk to God.

How long over time should you pray?

So, then, how long should you pray for something before giving up? The short answer is: Pray for something until either your prayer is answered or the circumstances change, making that prayer no longer appropriate.

I have heard many people say that they prayed for the salvation of a relative for 10, 20, 30 or more years. And in many cases the relative was saved eventually. So pray without giving up.

Give your burden to the Lord.

One of the benefits of prayer is that we can not only tell God about our cares, which he already knows, but we can formally turn them over to God to worry about. Asking for God's help puts the care on him, allowing us to be freed from worry about the remedy or outcome of the issue we've brought before his throne.

†
📖

Cast your burden upon the LORD and He will sustain you.

—Psalm 55:22a (NASB)

Our problem is that we too often take the burden back and continue to worry about it again, rather than feeling confident that it is in the Lord's hands now. The remedy is to keep putting the burden on God. Give it to him, and when you find yourself taking it back, give it to him again. Give and take back, give and take back, until the prayer is answered in a way that the burden is gone forever, or until you are successful in no longer taking it back again.

ဢ 🕊 ဢ
A PRAYER RETURNING THE BURDEN TO GOD

Dear Father, once again I have begun to worry and even agonize over [the issue]. That means I have taken the burden back from you and started to bear it myself again. Forgive me, Lord, for my weakness and humanness in doing so. I am just so concerned. Nevertheless, once again I place this burden into your strong and loving hands, knowing that you will take it on and that you will do your perfect will in handling it. May I always trust you with my worries and may you give me peace of heart in all things. I thank you and ask this in Jesus' name. Amen.

How long should your public prayers be?

There's a story about a preacher who went on and on with his sermon, piling point on point, illustration on illustration, and Scripture on Scripture. After a couple of hours, his notes were exhausted and his creativity had stopped. So, after he made one more highly emphatic point, he took a deep breath and said, "What more can I say?"

Quickly, someone in the audience said loudly, "Say Amen and sit down."

This story applies to public prayers as well. The fact is, people lose attention when they have to process a long stream of words. The brain basically tunes out the discourse because it can't handle so many words at once. (The same is true of lectures, business presentations, and narrated tours.) The live performance that runs too long causes lapses in attention as the brain seeks to catch up to what's already been said, so that new information is compromised, while at the same time the brain does not have the time and concentration to cement the previous information into long term memory. The short take: You hear only half of what is said and remember none of it.

Don't be overly concerned about the elegance of a public prayer. Make your point directly and plainly, and then say Amen. (But do consider adding figures of speech to clarify and enhance your message. See Chapter 16.)

ഩ 🕊 ഌ
A PUBLIC PRAYER FOR A MEAL

Dear Lord, we are so grateful that you have brought us together for fellowship with each other, and we thank you joyfully for the food we can share together. Bless this food to nourish and strengthen our bodies, and guide us to serve you with the energy it gives us. In Jesus' name. Amen.

ઠળ 🕊 ભ
ANOTHER PUBLIC PRAYER FOR A MEAL

Thank you, Lord, for enabling us to pause in our work and turn to you, the giver of all good things. We thank you and praise you for life, health, friends, and now especially, this abundant food. Bless this meal to the energizing of our bodies, and bless our hearts with the energizing of your Holy Spirit. May we serve you better as a result. In Jesus' name. Amen.

Advice for those new to prayer.
If you're new to the faith, or if you are a lifelong Christian who has always found prayer difficult, here are some ideas to help you.

1. Think about what you want to say and make notes. Some people think this recommendation is un-spiritual or awkward, but seasoned believers often keep and pray from prayer journals (see example pages in Chapter 17).

2. When you pray, invite the Holy Spirit to help you. That is one of his roles.

✝
📖

In the same way the Spirit also helps our weakness; for we do not know how to pray as we should, but the Spirit Himself intercedes for us with groanings too deep for words; and He who searches the hearts knows what the mind of the Spirit is, because He intercedes for the saints according to the will of God.
—Romans 8:26-27 (NASB)

3. Begin every prayer with thanks, no matter what your present circumstances. Whenever you talk to

God, find something to thank him for. It might be some blessing received today, an ongoing blessing you have been receiving over time, or a blessing given to you in the past.

If you are in such a challenging time in your life (perhaps suffering from chronic illness) that you find it difficult to feel a current blessing, think back in your past and thank God for a blessing you enjoyed then but didn't recognize it as a blessing. For example, now that I can't smell much of anything anymore, I thank God that I enjoyed a keen sense of smell for the first 50 or so years of my life. We express retrospective gratitude when we think back with new thanksgiving on something we now realize was a blessing but at the time we took for granted. We express appreciation to God for our having had something that is no longer present. Chronically ill and older people sometimes find it easier to remember blessings from the past than current blessings.

It is sometimes said that we never value (or are grateful for) many of our blessings, which we take for granted—until we lose them. When was the last time you thanked and praised God for the gift of eyesight, or hearing, or your sense of smell? Do you take your car for granted? What about your children? Are you thankful that you can eat regularly or afford all the potato chips you want?

4. Subject every request to God's will. Just as in the Lord's prayer, we ask for God's will rather than ours to be done in the case of any conflict or incompatibility. We have a tiny outlook on what we think is the most desirable outcome for a given situation, but God sees everything, everywhere, now and in the future. He sees through the fog that limits our seeing what's ahead. Trusting God's actions and his answer to our requests makes a lot of sense.

5. Make your request with humility. There is a saying, "Give people a handout and they will take it with gratitude; give them a second handout and they will take it as an expectation; give them a third handout and they will take it as an entitlement." The fact is, with God, every gift is undeserved. No answer to prayer should be viewed as an expectation, an entitlement, or a demand. Remind yourself that what you really want is God's answer, so that the best outcome will result.

6. Give praise to God for who he is. God should be loved for being a loving and generous being, not because of the amount of stuff he gives you or the number of prayers he answers the way you want them to be answered. We should always pray, "May you be forever exalted in my life and in the lives of my family, and may your infinite wisdom prevail always."

ഌ 🕊 ര
A MODEL PRAYER

Dear Father, I praise your name and your generous hands, that bless me beyond what I can ever want or need. Thank you for allowing me to live such a comfortable, easy life. As I go out today to [do some task], I pray that you will guide my efforts and help me as I work. May I be successful in achieving my goal with your help. And may everything this day reflect your will and your glory. In the name of Jesus I pray. Amen.

ಬ 🕊 ಌ
ANOTHER MODEL PRAYER

Dear God, you have been with me through every event in my life, all blessings except for a few challenges. I praise and thank you for the many, many blessings. And I praise and thank you for the challenges, too, for they have held my ego in check and taught me important lessons about life. Now I face another challenge. It's a big storm, a storm where I can't see the shore on the other side. So I really need your help. Please, Lord, may it be your will to work a miracle here and calm the waters. Or if it's your plan that I must ride it out, please be my helmsman and steer me through safely. Whatever happens, you are my God, and I love you and trust in you. I pray in the name of Jesus, who demonstrated your care for me by willingly suffering torture and death to pay for my sins. Amen.

✠✠✠

Chapter 8 Questions for Thought and Discussion

1. Think about how you pray. Do you pray several times a day with short prayers or once or twice a day with longer prayers? Do you tend to pray ad hoc — wherever you are, whatever you're doing, or do you pray more formally, in your "prayer closet" or dedicated time and place? Have you tried changing your prayer practice to see if another method improves your fellowship with God?

2. Do you adopt the same posture each time when you pray or do you have different ones? Have you tried the more submissive postures such as kneeling, or clasping your hands and bowing your head? Do

you notice a difference in the communication when you do this?

Chapter 8 Activities

1. Make a list of the people and things you pray for. Next, write a one-minute prayer for your top five. (Feel free to do more than five if you want.) Take these prayers with you and take the opportunity to pray one of them whenever you have to wait, such as waiting for a dentist appointment, for a meeting to start, for a movie to begin, for your computer to start up, for the water in the shower to get hot, and so forth. After a week or so, assess your reaction. Has the experience been positive? Has it improved your relationship with God? Has it helped your prayer life? Has it helped those you are praying for?

2. If you have difficulty praying publicly, create a plan for overcoming this spiritual shyness. Begin by planning to say grace when you eat out with one other person. Then, say grace when you are out with two or three others. Next, offer to pray in your small group or Sunday School class. Finally, at the next retreat, campout, or large meeting, offer to pray for others or some part of the world situation. It's not necessary to pray ex tempore; you can use notes or even a script. (If you do write a script, go over it repeatedly and practice using a new, lively tone of voice. Hide the fact that it has been written earlier.)

Chapter 8 Group Activities

1. Have each member of the group share the answers to these questions:

- Do you prefer to pray alone or with someone else? Why?
- Which posture do you usually adopt when praying? Name the other postures you sometimes employ. Explain your decision-making rules on how or why you change postures.
- How long are your typical prayers? Explain why they are the length they are.
- Do you pray for everything at once (yourself, others, world issues, etc.) or do you divide your prayers by theme or subject?

2. Discuss as a group the issue of giving your cares and burdens to God and then taking them back and worrying over them again. What are some of the remedies or solutions that have been tried and that have been successful?

3. Jesus prays at length in John Chapter 17. Read his prayer and discuss why he prayed at such a length.

9

How Does God Answer Prayer?

> *God answers all our prayers. Sometimes the answer is yes. Sometimes the answer is no. Sometimes the answer is, "You've got to be kidding!"*
> — *Jimmy Carter*

Yes, God answers every prayer. If you think about it, though, you can understand why he doesn't answer every prayer with a Yes, immediately. Suppose, for example, that John prays, "Lord, I need rain on my field right now," and Jim standing ten feet away prays, "Lord, please keep the rain away while we finish putting on my house's new roof." God isn't going to answer both prayers with an immediate Yes. But since he does answer every prayer, the question is, How does he do it? How does God answer prayer? There are many ways and many answers.

1. Yes, certainly. Here you are.

The answer we all hope for is the simple, "Yes, here you are." We think we know what's best for ourselves and others, so we hope God will give an instant positive answer to our request. This is the answer we all think we want, and are happy to get. God loves to give us what we need, and when our requests align with his will, he often grants the prayer. We're more likely to get a Yes answer when we study God's word and come to know his will for our lives and the lives of others.

✝

📖

Isaac prayed to the LORD on behalf of his wife, because she was barren; and the LORD answered him and Rebekah his wife conceived.
— Genesis 25:21 (NASB)

And God knows what's good for us and for those we pray for. And what's best for us is not always what we are praying for. That's why all of our prayers should include "if it's your will," or "may it be done according to your will."

Because we are so limited in our experience and understanding, we often ask for the wrong things at the wrong time. This explains why this simple "Yes, right away" answer is often so rare.

But life is more complex than we can ever know. At a bowl game somewhere, half the stadium is praying for one team to win, while the other half of the stadium is praying for the other team to win.

Takeaway:

Always ask for God's will.

2. Yes, but only because you insist.

Sometimes, we ask and ask and ask for something before God finally gives in. The answer might be, "Yes, but I wish you'd prayed for my will because you're going to regret this." Sometimes God lets us make a mistake in order to teach us that our own will is deeply tainted: We're self-centered, self-interested, self-serving—even though at the time we are convinced that we're being so selfless.

Takeaways:

Don't try to wear God down by grinding away with unending begging.

When you ask for something from God, be sure you are ready to receive the answer.

Note well: God already knows what you want and what you need (which are often two different things). Submit your requests to God, and then ask for his will rather than yours. It might not be pleasant if God answers your insistent prayer with a Yes, only as a means of demonstrating to you the folly of your request.

3. Yes, but you aren't paying attention.

Sometimes God answers our prayer with Yes, but we don't recognize it because we have a predetermined idea about what that Yes answer will look like. So, when you pray, look around you and think: Did God answer Yes already and I just need to look around and see it? Is the answer right in front of me if only I can understand it?

God doesn't always provide a Yes answer in a form we recognize immediately. The answer to our prayer might be staring us in the face, but since it's not in the form we requested and expected, we don't recognize it.

NOT PAYING ATTENTION

"Hey, Carlos."

"Hey, Manny."

"What's going down?"

"Nothing. I've got car problems — and God problems."

"What do you mean?"

"My car is still choking on that bad gas I got. Last night it wouldn't start."

"That's a car problem. What's your God problem?"

"Same thing. Last night was the prayer meeting. I prayed to God that my car would start so I could get there, but the answer was, 'No.' I cranked and cranked and prayed and prayed until the battery went dead."

"So you missed the prayer meeting?"

"No, Ted and Sarah happened by just as I was giving up on my car. They were on the way to the meeting and gave me a ride."

"That's great."

"Yeah, but I still don't know why God doesn't answer my prayers. I guess he just doesn't pay attention to me."

Takeaway:

**God sometimes answers the *What*
with a different *How*.**

4. Yes, but a little at a time.

That's right. Sometimes God is a serial answerer. He gives us an answer divided into several parts, perhaps waiting between parts to make sure we can handle each part — or to observe how well we do handle each part.

Let God take his time in answering your requests. You needed time to raise your kids to prepare them for the world; and so too God takes time in preparing you for heaven—not because he needs it, but because you do.

Takeaway:

Be patient with God as he is patient with you.

5. Yes and No.

Sometimes God grants part of our request but not all of it.

Suffering Humanity

Arnie opened the envelope enthusiastically, but his grin turned into a frown as he read the letter. "Oh, man!" he said. "Is God hard of hearing or something?"

"What's your problem this time?" asked Ed, his friend.

"I prayed for a week that God would let me go on that missions trip to Europe—England, France, Spain, and Italy."

"And? You're out?"

"No, but all I got was three weeks in England."

"Air travel, transportation, housing, food, and supplies all covered by the Missions Board?"

"Well, yeah. So?"

"I can see why you're depressed. Life is just a constant, agonizing grind for you, isn't it? Here, I'm luxuriating in the sun, framing houses all day in the 102-degree heat, and while I'm so lucky as to get a sunburn and a backache, you're condemned to suffer through three weeks of an all-expenses-paid trip to England. Yes, God must really dislike you."

"But God didn't answer my prayer. I wanted Europe and all I got was England."

Takeaway:

Count your blessings.

6. Yes, but only temporarily.

Remember that the purposes of life are to serve God, to grow spiritually (moving toward sanctification) and to help bring others into the kingdom and nurture them along the way. It is sometimes the case that to further these ends, an answer to prayer might be only temporary or for a season.

STILL LOVED AFTER ALL THESE YEARS

"I guess God has given up on me," Hank said, sadly.

"What are you talking about?" said Norm, Hank's best friend. "You have always been super blessed, if I may say so. You've got a great house, a good job, a wife much better than you deserve, and two normal kids. So what on earth are you whining about?"

"Well, for many years, I've always included in my prayers that God would give me good health."

"And it looks to me like you've always had it. Don't tell me they've raised your gym membership fees."

"It's not that."

"Okay, spill it."

"I've got cancer."

"Oh, I'm so sorry, buddy. That stinks."

"So you see why I'm saying that God has given up on me. He isn't answering my prayers for health."

"Look, Hank. The fact that God has kept you healthy for—how long now?—sixty-five years?—certainly must let you know that he cares dearly for you."

"But—."

"And now that he's changed one answer to *No* so that you can have a new adventure glorifying and trusting him, you shouldn't take that as some kind of blanket abandonment."

"But I—"

"And, as you know, God allows things to happen that he doesn't appoint. After all, the Bible says that God wants everyone to be saved, but not everyone is."

"I guess that's true."

"But, hey, I'm so sorry you've come down with cancer. We can now enter a new area of prayer for you, for healing."

"Thanks, Norm. You're not as bad a guy as everyone says."

"You, too, Hank. I love ya, buddy."

Takeaway:

Celebrate the season.

7. Yes, but not quite what you asked for.

Sometimes God's answer to your prayer is Yes, but it's something a bit different from what you had in mind. Sometimes he answers the prayer you would have prayed if you had known all the facts or circumstances—or possibilities. Remember that God can see down the road and around the corner, while we can see only what's in front of us—and that in a mirror dimly.

HOW ABOUT SOMETHING DIFFERENT?

"Hello, Fran? This is Jane next door."

"Oh, hi Jane. Seems like we never get to talk. What's the news in the Frimble household, and how is Vincent?"

"Oh, we're all fine. But excuse the rush. I have a pressing problem. The garbage disposal has gone bad. It hasn't been grinding well for a while and now it's started to leak under the sink. All this and I need to cook for my Faith Group coming over to-morrow. Do you know a reliable plumber who can come out right away? I've been praying for one, but so far nothing. The ones I've called say they are backlogged for a week. God doesn't seem to care."

"Well, Jane, it just so happens that Hank has practically made a career out of changing disposers. He's put three in our house over the years, and who knows how many in relatives' houses."

"But how much—."

"Don't worry about paying him. He loves to use his tools. Men are like that. Just reimburse him for the disposer. He's home now. Shall I send him over?"

"Wow. When God doesn't answer our prayers, the neighbor does. That's great."

"No, Jane. That's God."

†

📖

…for all things are possible with God.
—Mark 10:27b (NASB)

Takeaway:

Pray for God's answer, not necessarily yours.

✝
📖

Now we see things imperfectly, like puzzling reflections in a mirror, but then we will see everything with perfect clarity. All that I know now is partial and incomplete, but then I will know everything completely, just as God now knows me completely.
—1 Corinthians 13:12 (NLT)

As the saying is,

Only God knows all the options.

Sometimes we think we have a choice only between A and B, so we pray for one of them. But God knows there are also options C, D, and E. He also knows that, if we had known about them, we would have prayed for, say, E. So after we ask for A or B, he gives us E, which is what we really wanted but didn't know it.

As it has been said many times, God can see around corners while we can barely see in a straight line.

8. Yes, plus.

This is the Ephesians 3:20 answer, "beyond what you can ask or think." God not only gives you a favorable answer, but he does so in a glorious, sumptuous manner. Things you never thought to want are amazingly included with the Yes answer.

†

📖

I want you to desire the best gifts. So I will show you a much better way.
— 1 Corinthians 12:31 (CEV)

THE BLESSING UPGRADE

"Hello, sir. Welcome to Doaxtronix. How may I help you?"

"You have the Smervitz-Jorgensen XL4884dw printer on sale. I'd like to get one of those, please."

"Oh, I'm sorry, sir, but we just sold the last one."

"You did? And here I was praying for God's help in deciding which printer to buy and it seemed to be that one. Now I'm disappointed."

"Well, sir, we do have the S-J model XL6644dw multifunction machine, which has the same printing capability as the one you wanted, plus it has scanning, copying, and fax capability."

"Yeah? How much? I was looking at getting the XL4884 for $179."

"Well, the XL6644 just went on sale this morning for 40% off. Regular $229, this week, $138."

"Really!!???"

"And the toner is cheaper, too."

"Whoo eeee! God really knows how to deliver!"

"So do we, sir. So do we."

†

📖

Now all glory to God, who is able, through His mighty power at work within us, to accomplish infinitely more than we might ask or think.
— Ephesians 3:20 (NLT)

Takeaway:

**God is free to substitute a better answer
than the one you requested.**

9. Yes, but are you sure?

Sometimes God wants us to show that we are really serious about what we are praying for. Have we really thought this request through, or is it something that just occurred offhand and that we will lose interest in soon? Remember that God already knows what we want and what we need, so our prayers are at least in part for our own benefit, to let us and God know how earnest, committed, focused, and prioritized we are. If you are willing to keep praying for something for a while, God knows then that you are really serious. But if you stop praying or replace your request with something else, you will demonstrate less of a commitment.

COMMITTED

"This is such a great store. They have so much cool stuff here," said Melanie as she and Sheila entered.

"I know. I know. Ooh, look here at the sale flyer. They have a Blu-ray player."

"May I help you ladies?"

"Yes," said Sheila. "I want one of these Blu-ray players."

"We've sold a bunch of those. But I'm not sure we have any left. Want me to check?"

"Oh, yes please."

"Okay. I'll be right back."

"Oh Lord," Sheila said, scrunching her eyes closed and clenching her fists, "please let there be one in stock for me."

After Sheila opened her eyes, Melanie said, "Hey, Sheila. Look! They have a whole TV with a built-in Blu-ray player for just $40 more than the player you wanted."

"Oh, Lord," Sheila said, once again scrunching her eyes closed and holding on to the TV, "never mind my previous prayer. Instead, let there be one of these TVs in stock."

Just then, the salesman returned, holding a boxed Blu-ray player. He was about to say that after some hunting, he had found the very last one, when Sheila sent him off in search of the sale TV.

"Ohh, Sheila," Melanie said, "look at the super happening jacket I got from the Closeout rack!"

"Aww, I want that," said Sheila. "Do they have another one?"

"I didn't see one, but let's go look."

"Yeah. Oh Lord, forget my last prayer. Just let there be one more of these jackets in my size. Please, please, please. Thank you!"

That's a simple example, but the point remains for other requests, too. If you are praying for something big, such as whether to buy a house, change jobs, get married, or invest an inheritance, you might need to pray for some time and enlist others to join you. If you just pray once when you first hear about the situation, God may suspect you are less serious than you should be.

Takeaway:

Before you ask, think it through.

10. Yes. Now get started.

Everyone agrees that God frequently uses people to answer prayers. He doesn't always perform a miracle or use his own power to produce the answer to our requests. His answer often comes through the presence, wisdom, or even physical action of humans like ourselves.

What you might find surprising is that the person chosen by God to answer your prayer, in whole or in part, is sometimes you yourself. When you pray, then, let God take the burden on himself to worry about your need, but don't be surprised if you become part of the solution. Guidance from the Lord is in itself a precious answer to prayer. And as for action, you just might be the most efficient way for God to say Yes.

THANK YOU FOR YOUR SUPPORT

"Hey, George. I see the tarp is off your roof."

"Yeah, I finally got my roof fixed."

"Praise God."

"Not so much. I finally got tired of praying and waiting, so after seven months, I finally fixed it myself."

"Praise God. Prayer answered."

"What are you talking about? Didn't you hear me? I prayed for seven months that God would fix my roof, and then I gave up and fixed it myself. God had nothing to do with it."

"Hmm. Roof leaks at point A. George prays at point B. Roof doesn't leak at point C. Therefore, prayer answered. Praise God."

"But I fixed it."

"So? Do you object to being God's subcontractor? Don't you pray every day to be a better servant and to do God's will? Your prayer was for a fixed roof and now you have one. Praise God. Prayer answered. Thank God."

"But if I fixed it myself, how is that an answer to prayer?"

"Was your prayer for a fixed roof?"

"Well, yeah."

"And?"

"Okay, okay. I get it. Still, it seems kind of weird to have to answer my own prayer. Cost me almost a hundred dollars for materials, too."

"You're such a grateful Christian, George."

Takeaway:

Don't be surprised when God chooses you to answer your prayer, in part or whole.

11. No.

Sometimes the answer is No. And that's a good thing. When God answers our request with a No, we should be just as grateful as when he answers with Yes. If your child asks you for a drink from a bottle of drain opener, you say No because you know that's not good for the kid. In the same way, some of the things we ask for we shouldn't. Sometimes down deep we know we shouldn't be asking for something particular, but other times we ask in ignorance.

And there are many times when our requests are selfless and compassionate, as when we pray for a friend's healing. And yet the answer is No. In these cases, we must put our trust in God's wisdom and God's love, remembering that he sees everything and knows everything. And, of course, we need to remind ourselves that our real home isn't here on this fallen planet anyway.

✝
📖

For who has known the mind of the Lord? Or who has been His counselor?

— Romans 11:34 (HCSB)

Takeaway:

**Before you pray,
prepare your heart for God's will.**

12. No, but maybe if you refocus.

God knows when we need to rethink what we are asking for before he gives us a favorable answer. Sometimes we are just thinking in the wrong direction, or putting the wrong interpretation on something. Result: Praying for the wrong problem. Until we think things through and refocus our prayer, God won't budge.

BE TRANSFORMED BY THE RENEWING OF YOUR MIND

"Hey, Lissa. You look like you could use a cup of coffee."

"Thanks, Teek. I'm okay."

"Too much work?"

"No. Actually it's Neda."

"Neda? She seems harmless enough. And she has such interesting issues."

"Yeah. Interesting issues, all right. But that's the problem. She never stops telling me her problems. She's in my office half the day venting, crying, and complaining to me with tale after tale of her former, current, and future issues."

"Wow. Talks that much, huh?"

"You don't know the half of it. If I had a nickel for every problem she's complained about, I'd now be the owner of a private island in the tropics."

"Ooh, a private — ."

"And the problem is, I've prayed over and over that God will either resolve her problems or keep her away from my office and find her another audience to steal time from."

"I feel sorry for both of you, Lissa. But don't send her to me. I've got work to do."

. . . .

"Hey, Lissa. Long time no see."

"Hi, Teek. What's up?"

"My, you seem a lot happier than the last time I saw you. Did someone finally talk herself to death?"

"You mean Neda? Actually, we've become friends."

"Friends? With Neda? What happened?"

"I finally changed my prayers from 'Please help me to get rid of Neda' to 'Please help me to help Neda.'"

"And God answered your prayer?"

"Yes, he did. It started when Neda and I went to lunch, where she confided in me about some real underlying issues. And I have been able to help her."

"Oooh. What kind of underlying issues? Sounds delicious."

"Sorry, Teek. I don't gossip."

"Oh, Lissa. You're no fun."

When we've prayed a long time for something and haven't gotten an answer, we sometimes need to do some soul searching, revise our prayer, and ask for something else or even for God's will instead of our own.

Takeaway:

**God's perspective,
and therefore his answer,
is best.**

13. No, and here's something to think about.

This answer might be given when you pray for something inappropriate and do so repeatedly. If your prayers reflect the mindset of an ignorant, selfish child or an all-too-well-informed selfish adult, you might expect a loving tap from the hand of God instead of a Yes. If you do get such a response, think about it carefully, long, and deeply. It comes from a loving Father. Remember the Scripture:

†
📖

And you have forgotten the exhortation which is addressed to you as sons, "My son, do not regard lightly the discipline of the Lord, nor faint when you are reproved by him; for those whom the Lord loves he disciplines, and he scourges every son whom he receives."
—Hebrews 12:5-7 (NASB)

Takeaway:

Ask why you ask.

14. No, but you'll thank me later.

The longer you live in the life of prayer, the more opportunities you'll have to look back and thank God for answering certain prayers with a No. Once again, had you known all that God knows, you never would have asked for that. At the time, it's disappointing or even incomprehensible when the answer is No, but a few days, weeks, or even years down the road, you'll see that God really does care about you.

Sad to say, sometimes we will have to get our explanation directly from God when we get to heaven, because a part of this No is, "You won't understand why until I can explain it in person."

He Holds the Future

"Hello?"

"Hi, Sandy. It's Julie."

"Oh hi, Julie. How are you?"

"More to the point, how are you?"

"Why? What do you mean?"

"I'm sure you've heard they arrested Dan Umber."

"Dan Umber? Really?"

"Yeah. He's been beating on his wife and kids. For a long time apparently."

"That's terrible."

"Yeah. Never seemed to be able to hold down a decent job. So he drank and took it out on the family."

"But why are you telling me this?"

"Weren't you in deep love with Dan in college?"

"That was just a crush."

"A crush, huh? Don't I remember many, many nights where you sat on my bed and bawled your eyes out, in between begging God to make Dan love you?"

"No, I, I —."

"And you were so mad at God for such a long time, too. Guess he knew something you didn't."

"Julie —."

"Maybe you should make up with God. And maybe your hubbie Phil wasn't such a bad choice, either."

"Thanks for the call, Julie —."

"Better give him a special hug of gratitude when he gets home, don't you think?"

"Gotta go. My soup is boiling over."

Takeaway:

Sometimes a No
becomes a No? Thanks!

15. No, and stop being ridiculous.

Have you ever prayed for something that, in retrospect, seemed foolish or immature? Or have you ever done something you knew was wrong or harmful, but prayed to be kept safe from the consequences? And did you expect God to stop laughing long enough to answer that prayer with a Yes?

Do you realize that if God did answer Yes, he would be complicit in your folly?

There's an old saying that I just made up: If you accidentally get between a mother bear and her cub, ask God to deliver you, but if you grab the cub and slap it around a bit, don't ask God for anything. Just tell him you're on the way.

The wise person, upon receiving an answer like this, understands why the answer was No, and repents from asking for such a wrong or even sinful thing. The unwise person blames God for not answering the prayer. If you think about every No answer you receive, you'll have a great opportunity to increase your spiritual wisdom, especially if you do it in conjunction with reading the word of God in the Bible.

ဨ 🕊 ♋

A PRAYER FOR WISDOM IN PRAYING

Dear God, I come to you in love and worship, glorifying your name and praising your love. When I think about how great you are and how little I am, I am humbled and grateful that you pay any attention to me and my prayers. I know you listen and I know you respond. Lord, I always need your help and guidance in many things, and I always will. But I also need your wisdom to know what to ask you for. Please help me to be wise and mature in my requests, and regardless of what I pray for, always do your will when you answer. Keep me from selfish, foolish, and harmful requests. And may you be honored in my whole life. In Jesus' name. Amen.

Takeaway:

**If the answer is No,
take another look at the question.**

16. Wait.

Sure, we are all impatient to have our prayers answered right away. But for God's purposes—and often for our own growth—the answer is sometimes Wait. And it might be Wait a Long Time. Look at some of the Biblical characters—Joseph was in jail for two years before he was called to interpret Pharaoh's dream, and Abraham was a pretty old man before Isaac was born.

You've heard the old joke, "God give me patience and give it to me immediately." We live in a culture of instant gratification, so we expect instant answers to our prayers. And instant answers can happen. But commonly we are asked to wait upon the Lord and his good timing. Life seems to be a series of lessons in patience, for all of us. As the saying is, "When it comes to patience, we are all God's patients."

✝
📖

Dear friends, don't let this one thing escape you: With the Lord one day is like a thousand years, and a thousand years like one day.

—2 Peter 3:8 (HCSB)

THE PATIENT

"Hello, Christina. I didn't know you shopped this far from your office."

"Hi, Jan. Yeah, I wanted to get this book, *How to Develop Patience*."

"Ooh. Sounds interesting. Is it good?"

"Well, I skimmed it during lunch, but the guy wouldn't get to the point, so I'm going to return it. And this after I went through that parking lot nightmare with unbelievably slow drivers and foot-dragging pedestrians. And the checkout line—don't even talk about it."

"How long did you read the book?"

"At least half an hour. Well, maybe fifteen minutes."

"Why the anxiety, Christina?"

"I'm meeting a guy for dinner, so I have only four hours to develop patience. They say he's big on that."

"And did you pray about it?"

"No, God always takes too long to answer. I don't have time for that."

When you don't get a Yes answer after a while, how long should you wait before you give up? Jesus has the word about this:

✝

📖

Keep asking, and it will be given to you. Keep searching, and you will find. Keep knocking, and the door will be opened to you.
— Matthew 7:7 (HCSB)

Now, this is not a guarantee that if you keep asking, God will eventually answer with a Yes. You don't finally break down and give your kid a flame thrower just because he keeps asking long enough. But if you persevere in your asking, my guess is that the Lord will be much more favorably disposed to grant you what's in your best interest, the interest of others, and the interest of the kingdom.

And finally, Jesus himself again tells us "to pray always and not become discouraged" (Luke 18:1, HCSB).

Takeaway:

Add Patience to your prayer requests.

17. Wait, while I prepare you for a Yes.

You've heard that famous line, "You can't handle the truth." Sometimes when we pray for something, God knows that we can't handle a Yes answer. Not right now. So he lets us wait while he prepares a Yes or even a better answer for us.

Another way to look at this is to think about what a Yes answer might involve, including unforeseen events or circumstances. Perhaps a Yes answer will include some challenging issues that you need to prepare for. Such challenges could arrive right away or down the road. In either case, God is waiting while your heart develops the richness and strength that a Yes answer will require.

In a word, if the answer seems to be Wait, think your request through and prepare your heart.

Takeaway:

> **While you're waiting on God,**
> **study his word and grow in him.**

18. Here's something you didn't expect.

Sometimes God answers a prayer in a completely unforeseeable way. For example. you might pray, "Lord, let me know what to cook for dinner, and please put it on sale at the grocery store." And then ten minutes later you and your family are invited to a huge buffet at a friend's house.

Takeaway:

> **Don't be blinded by your own expectations**
> **about what an answered prayer will look like.**

19. Here's something you didn't even pray about.

And there is one final answer God gives to prayer, and that's the answer to a prayer you didn't think to pray. Sometimes an event will occur (an act of grace) that will be just what you wanted or needed, but you hadn't thought to pray about it. In hindsight, you say, "Thank you, Lord. That's just what I would have prayed for if I had thought to pray." This might be called the advance answer.

DON'T LET THE SUN GO DOWN

"Hi ya, Nat. What's up?"

"Oh, hi, Bren. Nothing's up. I'm just so stressed over the big blow up I had with Karen last Friday."

"Yeah, the grapevine says it was historic."

"You've heard gossip?"

"Have I? Whoo eeee!"

"The thing is, I actually like Karen and want to patch things up. I've been trying to get up enough courage to call her and hoping that she will accept my apology."

"For that to happen, you'll have to grovel big time. It would be best if you're sobbing when you call."

"I guess —."

[The phone rings.]

"Hello? This is Natalie."

[Over the phone:] "Hi, Natalie. This is Karen. I've been thinking about our misunderstanding last week, and I think we should just forget about it. Are you available for coffee this afternoon?"

Takeaway:

God knows what you need.

✠✠✠

Chapter 9 Questions for Thought and Discussion

1. Have you ever prayed, hoping for a Yes answer, only to get one of the other answers discussed in this chapter? If so, what was your reaction?

2. When you pray, do you always leave the answer to God's will? Explain why or why not.

3. When you pray for something and the answer is No, do you still have an "attitude of gratitude"? Explain why or why not.

4. Regardless of the type of answer, what makes every answer to prayer unique?

Chapter 9 Activities

1. Consider something you have prayed for in the past. For each one of the possible answers discussed in this chapter, write down what an answer to that prayer might have looked like. For example, what might a Yes, Plus answer have been? What about a Wait?

2. Think back on some of the things you've asked God to do for you and received what you thought was a No answer. Examine the list of answers given in this chapter. Were any of your requests apparently answered with one of these responses?

3. As you have probably experienced, the final answer to a prayer is not always evident right away. For example, what seemed to be a No might turn out to have been a Wait, followed by a Yes. Make a table similar to the one below that lists Apparent Answers in the left column and Later or Final Answers in the right column. Here are some sample entries get you going:

Apparent Answer	Final Answer
No	Wait
Yes	Yes, but only temporarily
No	No, but you'll thank me later
Yes	Yes, but not quite what you expected

Chapter 9 Group Activities

1. On a flip chart or marker board, write the numbers 1 through 25. Read each answer possibility corresponding to each number (with 20 to 25 for additions from the group) and ask for a show of hands from everyone who has experienced that answer. Discuss which answers are most and least common and explore why.

2. Ask group members to give examples of each of the various answers to prayer. If there are several examples of the same answer, discuss what they have in common and how they differ.

10

Emergent Prayers

Aspire to God with short but frequent outpourings of the heart; admire his bounty; invoke his aid; cast yourself in spirit at the foot of his cross; adore his goodness; treat with him of your salvation; give him your whole soul a thousand times in the day.
— *Francis de Sales*

Emergent prayers.

Emergent prayers are those arising from an immediate situation and are offered on the fly as you sometimes suddenly recognize a need to talk to God. The need to talk can involve

- a need for God's assistance, such as entering heavy traffic, trying to find something, or facing a pop quiz.
- a desire to thank God for an unexpected blessing, such as an appointment time much sooner than you expected, a gift from a friend, public praise from your manager, finding an address after the navigation system misled you, or a surprisingly good cup of coffee with your fast food order.

- a sudden impulse to praise God for who he is as a wave of joy sweeps across your heart.

As you can guess, emergent prayers can be quite informal and abrupt, as the situation warrants. Here are some examples:

಼ 🕊 ಚಿ

A PRAYER WHILE DRIVING

Lord, please help me to make this weave lane transition safely. Bring me a break in traffic if it pleases you. Thank you.

಼ 🕊 ಚಿ

A PRAYER WHILE WORKING

Lord, help me to get this screw started correctly. It doesn't seem to want to cooperate. I need your help. And once again I realize that I can't do anything without you.

಼ 🕊 ಚಿ

A PRAYER OF THANKS FOR A SMALL BLESSING

Thank you, dear Lord, for this parking place in such a crowded parking lot. I appreciate your kindness, and I recognize that I don't deserve it. Thank you so much in Jesus' name. Amen.

See Chapter 8, page 130 for more examples of emergent prayers.

Continual prayer.
When we develop the habit of sending small prayers to God at frequent intervals, we move into a state of

continual[4] prayer, where we constantly praise, ask, and thank God for all things.

It's as if God were a friend keeping us company, and we simply chat to him all day long, seeking advice and thanking him for the good company. And, of course, God is a friend, and much more than a friend.

Living in the presence of God.

Continual prayer does not mean continuous prayer, where all earthly silence must be filled with your voice; even if you pray silently, you soon might get tired of yourself. Instead, the continual—the frequently recurring prayers—produce a continuous—ongoing without stopping—relationship with God. This is what Brother Lawrence means about practicing the presence of God. He says,

> That we should establish ourselves in a sense of God's Presence, by continually conversing with Him. That it was a shameful thing to quit His conversation, to think of trifles and fooleries.
> —The First Conversation

Later, he says,

> That we might accustom ourselves to a continual conversation with Him, with freedom and in simplicity. That we need only to recognize God intimately present with us, to address ourselves to Him every moment, that we may beg His assistance for knowing His will in things doubtful, and for rightly performing those which we plainly see He requires

---

[4] Continual = frequently recurring. Continuous = occurring without stopping.

of us, offering them to Him before we do them, and
giving Him thanks when we have done.
— The Fourth Conversation

All kinds of issues, often requests for help or protection, are brought to the throne of God ad hoc, when
the perceived need or blessing comes to mind. Prayers
about a job interview, thanks for a meal, help with a
plumbing project, guidance for choosing which book to
read next, forgiveness for an unkind thought or word
that slipped out—these are all frequent examples
among those who cherish God's love.

With emergent prayers, you enter God's presence
immediately (or you are already are in his presence),
and deliver a quick request or praise message. Keeping
God active in everything you do creates a happier,
more Spirit-filled life.

ဆာ 🕊 ൙

A PRAYER FOR A LAPTOP COMPUTER

Lord, please help me find a good laptop computer
with the features I want and the performance I need,
and may it be one that I can serve you with for many
years. And may I find one at a good price. All in
your will, Amen.

ဆာ 🕊 ൙

A PRAYER TO REMAIN CALM

Dear God, help me to be calm at this upcoming
meeting. Send your Holy Spirit to illuminate my
heart and mind and to give me the words to say
when I speak. Let me know how to phrase my
comments and my answers and may the Spirit remind me of all the knowledge I have, so that I may
answer each question appropriately. May the pro-

cess and the outcome be to your glory and honor. In Jesus' name, Amen.

✞✞✞

Chapter 10 Questions for Thought and Discussion

1. What is the shortest prayer you ever made? Why did you pray it? Was it answered?
2. How often do you make an emergent prayer? Why do you typically make them?
3. Of the last half-dozen emergent prayers you made, what were their topics?
4. Do you find that emergent prayers draw you closer to God? Do they keep you close to God?
5. How often do you offer an emergent prayer for some blessing you might ordinarily take for granted or not necessarily notice? For example, a good cup of coffee, beautiful clouds, a smooth-writing pen, a software application.

Chapter 10 Activities

1. Think about the times you have made an emergent prayer in the past week or two , and as well as you can recall, make a list of them. Now think about the list and divide the prayers into half a dozen categories that fit your collection. (For example, requests for safety, guidance, decision making, protection, blessing of food, overcoming fear, etc.) How many of each category do you recall? Can you derive some meaning from the results? Do you pray more for guidance than protection? perseverance through a situation rather than delivery from a situation?

Chapter 10 Group Activity

1. As a group, discuss the kinds, lengths, and words used for various emergent prayers by each member. What are the commonalities? What are the unique features?

11

Established Prayers

Prayer is the wing on which the soul flies to heaven.
— Ambrose of Milan

Established prayers are given for set occasions, such as morning waking, meals, closing the evening, and so on. These prayers can be either spontaneous or written down and repeated — if done so carefully so that the person praying isn't just going through the motions.

Established prayers are somewhat longer, less abrupt, and more deliberately considered than emergent prayers. When a thoughtful decision needs to be made, or thanks for a blessing is appropriate, taking the time to enter a formal prayer time and to turn to established prayers is an excellent idea.

In the examples below, notice that each prayer is relatively brief, but time is set aside to praise and thank God as well as to make requests. These first two prayers show gratitude to God for allowing the person praying to wake up to another day on earth, even though the day might be hard. We are called to serve, and we should be grateful for each additional day of opportunity.

ಹಿ 🕊 ಜಿ

A PRAYER UPON ARISING

Good morning, dear Lord. Thank you for bringing me to the beginning of a new day. Please help me to spend the day wisely and may all that I do be pleasing to you. May your Holy Spirit give me the right words to use in every situation I encounter, so that I will honor you and be effective with what I say. And please protect me as I travel to all of my destinations. I bless you and thank you. In Jesus' name. Amen.

ಹಿ 🕊 ಜಿ

ANOTHER PRAYER UPON ARISING

Thank you, dear Lord, for giving me life itself and for calling me into your kingdom and to another day of service to you. Guide me today to honor you in all that I say, do, think, and write. Please grant me safe journeys as I travel from place to place, and may my appointments be successful as they serve and please you. Give me strength and health and may I model Christ accurately as others look on. I pray this with gratitude and in the name of Jesus. Amen.

This next prayer is a simple table grace, thanking God and reminding ourselves who gives us everything that sustains us.

ಹಿ 🕊 ಜಿ

A PRAYER FOR THE MORNING MEAL

Thank you, Lord, for blessing us with this food, in its quality and abundance. We accept it from your hands with humility and gratitude and pray that it will nourish our bodies, giving us the strength we need to perform the tasks of the day. In Jesus' name we ask. Amen.

Do you take a brief break to refocus after the chores, tasks, meetings, or just mental work of the first few hours? Don't forget to spend at least a few moments to talk to your creator:

A Prayer at Midmorning

Lord God, I come to you with gratitude and to bless your holy name for being with me in my day so far. Thank you for being sovereign in my life. May you always guide me in my efforts and show me your will among all the choices that I encounter. Please continue to be with me this day, and may I reflect the love and light of Christ to everyone I meet. In his name I pray. Amen.

Lunchtime offers a great opportunity to fellowship with likeminded believers, and to offer thanks for the company as well as the food:

A Prayer for the Noon Meal

Lord, we thank you so much for this opportunity we have for food and fellowship today. Be with us in our time together and may our conversation honor you and be a blessing to each other. Thank you now for this abundant food, which we receive, as with every good thing, from your loving hands. In the name of our Lord Jesus. Amen.

Some countries enjoy an afternoon break from work, a siesta, because the human mind and body have a tendency to get sleepy around two or three o'clock. In the industrial world, however, work goes on. What can be done, though, is to take a five-minute break, relax with a beverage, and remember the Lord:

ഇരു 🕊 ൕ

A PRAYER FOR THE LATE AFTERNOON

Dear Lord, I come to you at the tired time. My mind isn't as sharp as it was this morning, and my body is running down. So I ask you, Lord, to refresh my mind and body. Restore my energy and renew my thinking. Please give me also the spiritual strength and confidence I need, and help me to keep you with me in all that I do. For I can do all things through you who strengthens me. I joyfully pray in Jesus' name. Amen.

ഇരു 🕊 ൕ

A PRAYER FOR THE EVENING MEAL

Thank you, dear Lord, that we are able to enjoy this wonderful food. You truly do give us "our daily bread" in abundance, and we bless you for this gracious and generous gift. Please bless the hands that prepared this food for us, and help us to serve you in all we do. In Jesus' name. Amen.

ഇരു 🕊 ൕ

A PRAYER UPON RETIRING FOR THE NIGHT

Thank you, my precious Lord, for bringing me to a safe conclusion of the day. Thank you for every one of the challenges you helped me face and deal with, and thank you for the blessings and accomplishments you gave to me. Forgive me for any sins I have committed, knowingly or unknowingly, and remind me in the morning of any wrong I need to right. Bless and watch over those I love and help us all to have a good night's sleep. If it pleases you, may we all rise tomorrow morning refreshed and ready to spend another day in your service. I pray in the name of my savior, Jesus. Amen.

෨ 🕊 ໑
A PRAYER FOR AN AGE MILESTONE

My dear Lord, I come to you with both gratitude and humility. I'm grateful to you for allowing me to reach [number] years of life. I so appreciate all you have given to me, helped me with, and guided me through. I am deeply thankful for everything you've helped me to accomplish in the years you've blessed me with. And I humbly acknowledge that I couldn't have done anything without your gracious guidance. Thank you for being my God and seeing me through. I'm yours for whatever additional time it pleases you to give me. In Jesus' name. Amen.

෨ 🕊 ໑
A PRAYER FOR THANKSGIVING

Father, we come to you in this Thanksgiving season, with the deepest gratitude for blessing our lives so richly. We are grateful for your generous hand that has given us food and shelter and clothing and material goods way beyond our needs. And we are grateful to you for giving us our families where we can find love and belonging and growth and security.

Thank you for all you have given us, O Lord; thank you for all you have helped us with; thank you for all you have guided us through; and thank you for all you have protected us from. We appreciate the friends you have put in our lives, the wisdom you have put in our minds and the love you have put in our hearts.

But most of all we thank you for saving us from our sins and making us heirs to the kingdom of heaven through Jesus Christ. Truly you have done for us "beyond what we could ever ask or think." So we say thank you, thank you, Lord. In the name of Jesus we pray. Amen.

✟✟✟

Chapter 11 Questions for Thought and Discussion

1. Do you find the established prayers most useful as (1) prayers to pray as they are written, (2) models that you can tweak (with names or specifics, for example), or (3) as suggestions for complete prayers you write yourself, using some of the same concepts?

2. How do you generally react to printed (established) prayers?

A. They seem fake and it's awkward listening to them being read.

B. They are fine, just helps for the person praying.

C. I treasure them because they are usually better than a person's extempore prayers, and I can keep and reread them later.

Chapter 11 Activities

1. Use two of the established prayers as models to write your own prayers, either on the same or a different subject.

2. Make a list of prayer subjects not included in this book.

3. Write two prayers on a subject not included in those in this book. Choose your own subject or choose from: Child, son, daughter, husband, wife.

Chapter 11 Group Activities

1. Discuss as a group what makes a publicly read established prayer better or worse. How can the negatives be overcome? Examples:

A. Better written prayers?

B. Improved delivery, not so awkward reading?

C. Longer? Shorter?

2. Which of the above choices has the most possibility and why?

3. Below is an established prayer that is different from the other examples in this chapter because it is written in rhymed couplets. It might be called a poem prayer.

A. Have someone in the group read the poem prayer aloud.

B. As a group, discuss your response to the prayer. Is it effective? awkward? beautiful? clumsy? spiritually impactful? spiritually offensive?

෨ 🕊 ෬

A PRAYER OF GRATITUDE

Help me, O Lord, forever to recall
That everything I own, you gave it all.
The sum of what I know, you led me to;
Whatever I can do is done through you.
All that I am was crafted by your hand;
May I become whatever you command.
Thank you, Lord, for such amazing grace,
That even sinner me you dare embrace.

4. Now as a group, have someone read the prose version of the poem prayer below and then discuss the differences. Which do you prefer and why?

A PRAYER OF GRATITUDE

Dear Lord, help me always to remember that you are the giver of everything I own. You have helped me learn everything I know; and everything I have accomplished has been with your help and grace. In fact, who I am now is the result of your work in me—may you continue to shape my life. I praise your name with thanksgiving for all this grace and for choosing me to enjoy the mercy that saved me from sin.

12

Intercessory Prayer

When you pray, remember you're not the only one who needs God's help.
                    — Anonymous

Overview.

Intercessory prayer is usually thought of as prayer by one person on behalf of the request or need of another: "Pray for me," is a common intercessory request. Often, people think they don't know how to pray adequately or else think that the person they ask to pray for them is more likely to be heard (possibly because the person asked is viewed as more "spiritual"). When you pray for people like that, you are becoming their bridge to the throne of God.

When people ask you to join them in praying, your prayers add to their own prayers to open multiple lines of petition. You become a prayer partner with them. Often, several or even many people will join in together to pray for someone.

In a larger sense, someone can intercede for another person without that person making a request: If you see a homeless, mentally ill person talking to a stuffed

animal, you can take it upon yourself to pray — to intercede — for that person. Similarly, prayer partners can
join together, either formally or even without knowing
of their other partners, to pray for someone or something the Spirit has placed on their hearts. For example,
many Christians pray for the protection of government
leaders, such as the president. And many pray for the
protection of Israel.

Challenges of personally requested intercessory prayer.
From all of this we can understand that intercessory prayer includes a broad range of types: One praying
for one, many praying for one, many praying for
many, and so forth. The commonality is that the inter-
cessor is praying for someone else. And this fact raises
some challenges.

Here are some of the challenges related to praying
for someone else, together with a few comments on
possible ways to approach each challenge.

1. The requester won't tell you the problem. When
someone asks you, "Please pray for me," but won't go
into further detail, then the requester is probably too
embarrassed to be plain. The difficulty for you lies in
not knowing whether to pray for healing, guidance, assistance, or some other category. Moreover, it's prob-
lematic to ask God to help the person be successful
since you don't even know the moral status of the situation.

Possible approaches.

A. Ask for the general category: "Do you need
prayer for healing, guidance in a decision, courage to
resist temptation, or something else?" If the requester

is unwilling to be any more specific, pray at the level of generality of the request:

A PRAYER FOR A GENERAL NEED

Lord God, you know the need [person] has on [his/her] heart. I pray that you will minister to this need according to your all-knowing, perfect and wise will. You know best how to handle this need, so I pray you will take it into your sovereign consideration and bring resolution that will glorify you. And if it pleases you, may you in your awareness, deliver [person] from any harm in this situation. Thank you for being God and for taking charge in this request. In Jesus' name. Amen.

B. If the requester is willing to identify the category of the request, you can pray for help less vaguely, but still more generally:

A PRAYER FOR HELP WITH A RELATIONSHIP

Dear God, we come to you with thanksgiving for being our sovereign God as well as our caring friend. We ask today that you will be gracious in helping [person] with [his/her] relationship difficulties. Lord, we know that you desire reconciliation and harmony among all those who live to serve and to please you. Whatever the issues causing unhappiness between [person] and another or others, we ask that you will dissolve resentments, reveal misunderstandings, and work in the lives of everyone to come back together with mutual respect. We know that the situation is difficult and that everyone will face changes. So we ask for you to work through your

Holy Spirit to bring a positive and happy result. In Jesus' name. Amen.

2. The requester tells you something you think is not the real problem. Once again, if the real problem is too embarrassing to name, the requester might describe something else but related in an attempt to get you to pray in a way that will help cover the need.

Possible approach:

A. Ask questions, delicately. That is, ask, "What happened?" instead of, "What did you do that caused the problem?"

It's Complicated

"Alto, I'd like you to add my wife to your prayers."

"Of course, William. I'd be happy to. What's her need?"

"Well, she needs to keep her temper in check. Not lose her cool. I swear, she flies off at nothing."

"I see. Can you give me an example of when she has lost her cool?"

"Well, once when we were camping in the mountains, the soup pot spilled over and she yelled for ten minutes."

"I didn't know you two went camping."

"Well, this was just before we got married."

"Before you got married and had your four kids? I was thinking you might have a more recent example."

"Well, just the other night she lost her temper and yelled at me."

"Oh, that's too bad. Tell me about it."

"And in front of the two youngest darlings, too."

"What happened just before she yelled at you?"

"I spilled a little chip dip on the floor."

"How little?"

"The whole jar."

"Oh. How did that happen?"

"I was trying to balance a half gallon of ice cream on my head so I could get the two chip bags in one hand and the dip and a bowl in the other hand."

"And the dip jar broke?"

"Yeah, and she doesn't even like dip. And the bowl wasn't one of those pricey ones, either."

"It broke, too?"

"Yeah, fell right on top of the ice cream that fell out of the container. I thought the ice cream would have prevented the breakage."

"And then she started yelling at you? I think I can under—."

She started out laughing. So I told her to shut up—in a nice kind of way, you know—and then she went crazy and started yelling. She even used a couple of words they don't teach you in Sunday School."

"Tell you what, Will. I'll be praying for both of you."

"Thanks so much, Alto. I've been praying a lot myself for God to change her stony heart, but the Big Guy just doesn't seem to be listening."

3. The requester asks you to pray for something you object to.

Possible approaches:

A. Ask if the requester thinks that what is being asked runs against Biblical teaching. Cite Scripture that clarifies the situation. Tell the requester that praying for something God prohibits will not only be refused but God will be offended.

B. Following from A above or as a first response, ask some questions and see if you can alter the request into something you can pray for.

C. Offer to pray for the requester's heart and that the requester will seek God's will in everything.

4. You believe that the requester is the problem— and needs an attitude transplant rather than a change in the external environment or a change in other people.

Possible approaches:

A. Tell the requester that the only way to change others is to change yourself first. (This is a commonly used counselling concept.) When you pray, include only the requester and be careful not to make the prayer manipulative.

ഇ 🕊 ൙

A PRAYER FOR PERSONAL CHANGE

Dear God, we come to you with a difficult situation, Two of your children cannot get along or treat each other with kindness or respect. It seems that each blames the other for their hurt, and both are angry and resentful. Lord, I pray that you will lay a mantel of peace on both people in this situation and that you will help them turn their feelings and blaming and anger over to you. Then they can let it go and be set free. In the precious name of Jesus. Amen.

5. The request comes from a third party. "Pray for Bill because he's very sick." Much intercessory prayer fits into this category. We are (rightly) always praying for others, based on the need we can discover from the source, which is often not the ailing person.

Possible approach:

A. Pray categorically. Many times the intermediary will have a category of need to relate to you: "Pray for Jerome because he's having trouble with his marriage"; "Pray for Nancy because she has a surgical procedure on Wednesday"; "Pray for the Williams' son, who has a drug problem." Once you know the category, you know enough. You don't need to know the details before you can bring the issue to the Lord effectively. Remember, God already knows the issue in detail.

6. The need is unspoken. At a Sunday School meeting, at a Bible study, at a fellowship group, or any other meeting of Christians, the prayer leader often asks for participants to raise their hands if they have "unspoken needs." Often, too, the prayer leader will automatically include a request for help for those who have a need for prayer but who have not asked for it.

Possible approach:

A. This situation is quite similar to the one discussed in Issue #1, above, so it allows the same remedies.

ಶಿ 🕊 ೮ೖ
A PRAYER FOR UNSPOKEN NEEDS

Our heavenly Father, we thank you for being our generous, healing, forgiving, guiding Lord, who is eager to help us, that you may be glorified. We know that all of us have many needs, for we are weak and often misguided creatures. In addition to those we have prayed for with the needs they have declared, we now come to you to ask that you will minister to the unspoken needs of those here. Whether the need is physical healing, emotional comfort, financial help, or something else, we pray that you will take on these burdens, and bring relief from worry, and deliverance from the need. Minister to each and everyone here, and let them all experience the mighty helping hand of the Lord. All this we ask in accordance with your will and in the name of Jesus. Amen.

Challenges of intercessory prayer for an entity.

Most often, a person who requests prayer lets us know the issue involved. But when we discover the need for prayer for an entity — a nation, people group, legislative body, the survivors of an earthquake — the situation grows more complex. Here are some of the concerns.

1. The exact nature of the problem is unclear. For example, if you read that a tribal group in some land is suffering from disease and starvation, is the problem government isolation of the tribe, persecution by another tribe, religious warfare, poor soil for raising crops, ignorance of farming techniques, rule of the tribe by dictators with foolish ideas?

Possible approaches:

A. Do some research on the Web to find out more specifically what the problems facing the tribal group are. Then you can focus on praying for those specific needs or hindrances to prosperity.

B. Pray in general for the welfare and deliverance of that tribal group.

ℰ 🕊 ℭℛ

A PRAYER FOR HELP

Dear Lord, I come to you to ask that you will visit your gracious love and deliverance on the people of [country]. I have heard that they are suffering tremendously, and that many are diseased while others are starving. Lord, I don't know the cause of this evil, but you do, and so I ask you to bring about a remedy, a change, a blessing that will free these people from the horrible circumstances they are in. Please help them to obtain food and medicine. Thank you for listening to this request and for being a merciful God. In Jesus' name. Amen.

2. The solution to the problem is unclear or unknown. Sometimes, identifying the problem is not difficult—inner city street gangs, thousands of people dying each year from pain killer overdoses, domestic and international terrorism, abortion, murder—but identifying the solution seems, in many cases, to be almost impossible.

Possible approaches:

A. Become part of the solution. Do some research and find organizations that are fighting the evil. Pray for them, join them, support them, as well as the victims of the evil.

B. Pray that God, in his mercy and sovereignty, will do a mighty work in the area.

ಬ ⛪ ಞ

A PRAYER FOR GOD'S INTERVENTION

Father God, we are deeply troubled by the ongoing evil of [drug abuse, etc.]. You see it, Lord, and we know it burdens your heart as it does ours. We ask you, therefore, to take this destructive force into your mighty hands and break its power. Work in the hearts and minds of those who are or might be tempted to participate in this evil and help them to make a better choice. We also ask that you will send your Spirit to inspire every earthly authority to find and implement effective solutions, so that your suffering children can be delivered from the grasp of the Deceiver. We thank you and bless you in Jesus' name. Amen.

Public versus private intercessory prayer.

Jesus tells us to pray privately, for both our personal prayers and our intercessory prayers:

✝
📖

But you, when you pray, go into your inner room, close your door and pray to your Father who is in secret, and your Father who sees what is done in secret will reward you.

— Matthew 6:6 (NASB)

When you pray privately, you have the secret confidence of God. He never gossips. So, you can go into as much embarrassing detail as you want. When you pray in secret, you need not hold back. As mentioned before, God already knows the gory details.

When you pray for the needs of others in a public prayer, however, things change. Here are some guidelines:

1. Keep the prayer relatively brief. Lengthy intercessory prayers tend to become either laundry lists with too many people on them, or needlessly detailed.

2. Don't include details that might feed the gossip mill. You and your prayer group can agree on asking God for help without, say, detailing the requester's humiliating condition.

ဆ 🕊 ☙
A DISCREET PUBLIC PRAYER FOR HEALING

Lord God, we thank you for being the great healer, who can deliver us from our sicknesses through your mighty hand. We now bring Shauna before you with a need for healing. Please put your hand on her and deliver her from her condition. Heal her by your miraculous power, or give the doctors insight to apply the proper and effective medical treatment, and may it work quickly to free her from the discomfort she is now experiencing. This, with thanksgiving, we ask according to your will and in Jesus' name. Amen.

Now imagine sitting in your group and hearing the leader pray this way:

ဆ 🕊 ☙
AN INAPPROPRIATE PUBLIC PRAYER FOR HEALING

Dear Father in heaven, we come to you to ask your help with our physical needs. Please heal Shauna of her head lice, and bring healing to Janet from her urinary tract infection. Also, please heal Brad from his plaque psoriasis, and Tawna from her gum disease. [Et cetera.]

My recommendation, then, is that in public intercessory prayer, don't say too much.

The subjects of intercessory prayer.

The question sometimes arises, "Whom and what can we pray for?" As the hungry diner said as he handed the menu back to the waiter, "Yes." The world and its inhabitants are in—you guessed it—a world of hurt. Subjects of intercessory prayer can include:

- **An individual.** Spouse, child, grandparent, friend, pastor, coworker, enemy, president, governor, missionary, dictator, etc.
- **A people group.** Jews, Christians, those living under oppressive regimes, those in need of obedience to Christ and Scripture (atheists, Muslims, nominal Christians, cultists), etc.
- **Organizations.** Bible translators, Bible distributors in countries closed to the Gospel, Christian publications, churches, relief agencies, Congress, state government, etc.
- **Ideas and Ideals.** Justice, freedom, democracy, capitalism, truth, righteousness, obedience to Christ's commandments, the Christian worldview, etc.
- **An outcome.** A specific verdict in a trial, a Supreme Court decision, an election result, results in a competition, the outcome of an event, etc.

And remember, in intercessory prayer, public and private, as with every prayer containing a request, always submit your request as subject to God's will, trusting him for the best outcome.

APPOINTMENT

"Hi, honey."

"Hey, sweetheart."

"You sound a bit stressed. How did the interview go?"

"Okay, I guess. But I almost got there late."

"What happened?"

"Remember how you prayed, 'Lord, help Bill to have a safe and timely journey to the interview'"?

"Yes, and that God's will would be done in everything."

"Yeah, well, God had some strange plans for me. When I got downtown, my car broke down."

"Oh, no. What did you do?"

"Called a tow truck. I had to wait twenty minutes, my entire buffer time I allowed to be sure I got to the interview on time."

"Oh, I'm sorry."

"While I was waiting, I watched a homeless guy push a shopping cart full of empty soda cans all the way up Seventeenth Street."

"That's sad."

"Yeah. When he got to me, I gave him one of the blankets we keep in the car."

"What did he say?"

"He nodded and said, 'Cold.'"

"Poor guy."

"So finally the tow truck arrives and the driver takes his time hooking the car up."

"I can see why you got so stressed."

"So I'm riding in the cab with the driver, and I notice a picture of what's probably his family. When I comment on the picture, he starts telling me that his marriage is having problems."

"Oh, Bill, that's too bad."

"Yeah, well, when we got to the garage, I gave him a copy of *Marriage in a Nutshell* and told him that he and his wife should read and discuss it."

"Great job, honey."

"And then, one of the garage mechanics overheard my mention that the marriage book is partly based on proverbs from the Bible, so he came up to me and—long story short—asked me to pray for him."

"Wooo haah, as you men like to say."

"So I called a cab and got to the interview exactly on time. In fact, the admin told me they were waiting and that I should go right in."

"Wait a minute. Didn't you persuade the cab driver to pray the sinner's prayer, or something?"

"No the cab ride was just a cab ride. Uneventful. We talked about lawn mowers."

"Not even sharing the four spiritual laws?"

"Nope. Nada. Zip. But after the interview, I was asked to come back for a second interview with the big wigs."

"Honey, that's great. I'm so proud of you."

"Thanks, sweetheart. It just makes me wonder, though, why God didn't answer your prayer to give me a timely trip."

"I guess some things we won't know till we get to heaven."

✝
📖

Be still, and know that I am God.
— Psalm 46:10a (ASV)

✟✟✟

Chapter 12 Questions for Thought and Discussion

1. Do you spend more time praying for yourself or for other people? Why do you think that is the case?

2. Look at the list of subjects of intercessory prayer in this chapter. Which of the subject types do you pray for regularly? Which most? Which least? Which not at all?

3. How comfortable are you praying aloud with a group? If you are not comfortable, why do you think you aren't as relaxed as when you pray privately?

4. What is the point of the story that begins on page 192? Do you think that putting the point of the story into narrative form clarifies or obscures the point being made?

Chapter 12 Activities

1. If you are uncomfortable praying aloud, choose a short prayer, such as a blessing before eating, and read it aloud before a meal. If you are very nervous, follow this pattern:

A. Read the prayer aloud several times when you are alone.

B. Read the prayer aloud in the presence of one other person.

C. Read the prayer aloud when your whole family or several people are present.

D. Read the prayer aloud in a restaurant.

E. Pray the prayer, which by now you have memorized, following whichever steps in the above list are needed.

Chapter 12 Group Activity

1. Have each member of the group choose a prayer from this book and pray it aloud in front of the group.

A. After everyone has finished, discuss who felt comfortable and who felt uncomfortable, and discuss why.

B. Have those who felt uncomfortable pray the prayer aloud again, three or four times.

C. Discuss the results.

Bonus question. Compare the vignettes in this chapter or in the entire book with the parables Jesus told.

How do both aim at your memory, your heart, and your mind? Have you ever considered writing parables, vignettes, or skits that would present the Gospel in three dimensions?

13

Three Aspects of God's Will

> *The value of persistent prayer is not that he will hear us*
> *. . . but that we will finally hear him.*
> *— William McGill*

I have said how important it is when praying that we add, "if that is your will" to our requests, lest we end up asking for an outcome that is against God's purposes. It is also important to understand the nature of God's will so that we don't mistake why some things, especially bad things, happen. If we are to pray intelligently, we need to understand how God's will is involved in the events of our lives.

For example, when a disaster happens, is that God's will (or as the insurance companies like to say, "an act of God")? And if it is God's will, does that mean he wanted or planned for it to happen?

My view is that we mistake thinking that God's will is monothetic—that is, consisting of a single characteristic or aspect. I believe there are three different aspects to God's will. He has a preferential will, a permissive will, and an executive will. While all of these are his will, that is, things subject to his control, the aspects vary in the degree of determination God applies to the outcome.

God's preferential will.

God's preferential will represents those things he desires to happen or to be the case. This aspect of his will is his best plan or wish for our lives. This is the aspect of God's will we are referring to in our prayers:

✝
📖
May your will be done on earth as it is in heaven.
—Matthew 6:10b (NLT)

That is, may the events that occur on earth match the outcomes you want. May the things you prefer to happen be done. When we seek to know God's will for our lives, this is the aspect we seek, what he desires for us, what he wants us to do, his preferential will.

✝
📖
"For I know the plans I have for you," declares the Lord, "plans to prosper you and not to harm you, plans to give you hope and a future."
—Jeremiah 29:11 (NIV)

But people, with free will, can resist God's preferential will. A well-known example is that of Jonah:

✝
📖
Now the word of the Lord came to Jonah the son of Amittai, saying, "Arise, go to Nineveh, that great city, and call out against it, for their evil has come up before me." But Jonah rose to flee to Tarshish from

the presence of the Lord. He went down to Joppa and found a ship going to Tarshish. So he paid the fare and went on board, to go with them to Tarshish, away from the presence of the Lord.
—Jonah 1:1-3 (ESV)

Or consider the case of salvation. It is not God's preferential will that anyone should be lost:

✝
📖
The Lord is not slack concerning His promise, as some count slackness, but is longsuffering toward us, not willing that any should perish but that all should come to repentance.
—2 Peter 3:9 (NKJ)

On the contrary, it is God's expressed preferential will that everyone should be saved:

✝
📖
This [praying for those in authority] is good, and it is pleasing in the sight of God our Savior, who desires all people to be saved and to come to the knowledge of the truth.
—1 Timothy 2:3-4 (ESV)

But we clearly see that not everyone is saved. Many reject the Gospel and are lost, but this is against God's will—his preferential will.

In the parable of the lost sheep, Jesus tells us that God's preference is to keep everyone in the fold. He will go to extensive work to bring it in, but there is still an "if" in the circumstance:

†

📖

What do you think? Suppose a man has 100 sheep and one of them strays. Won't he leave the 99 sheep in the hills to look for the one that has strayed? I can guarantee this truth: If he finds it, he is happier about it than about the 99 that have not strayed. In the same way, your Father in heaven does not want one of these little ones to be lost.
— Matthew 18:12-14 (GW)

God's preference for our lives is exactly what we should be praying for when we ask him to let us know his will. His preferential will is his choice for us and for others, though we can resist it and do something else.

God's permissive will.

One of the great errors of popular theology is to blame God for every disaster and tragedy that occurs. Whenever something evil appears (accident, illness, death, war, famine, broken fingernail), immediately someone asks, "Why did God want this to happen?" This question results from a confusion about God's will, a confusion that conflates the three aspects into one entity.

The fact is that God allows many things to happen, both good and bad, that he does not appoint or order or even prefer. Just before he tells the parable of the lost sheep, quoted above (Matthew 18:12-14), Jesus acknowledges the presence and power of evil, and that evil occurrences are permitted, without having been appointed or approved by God:

✝

📖

But whoever causes one of these little ones who believe in me to sin, it would be better for him to have
a great millstone fastened around his neck and to be
drowned in the depth of the sea. Woe to the world
for temptations to sin! For it is necessary that temptations come, but woe to the one by whom the temptation comes!

—Matt 18:6-8 (ESV)

The moral and spiritual economy that God has established here on earth with humans who have been given
the gift of choice means that temptations—and giving
in to them—will happen, with the result that sin and
evil will be present. But that does not mean that God
desires, intends, or produces any of it, especially not
for punishment. Jesus specifically addressed this mis-
conception:

✝

📖

There were some present at that very time who told
him about the Galileans whose blood Pilate had
mingled with their sacrifices. And he answered
them, "Do you think that these Galileans were worse
sinners than all the other Galileans, because they
suffered in this way? No, I tell you; but unless you
repent, you will all likewise perish. Or those eight-
een on whom the tower in Siloam fell and killed
them: Do you think that they were worse offenders
than all the others who lived in Jerusalem? No, I tell
you; but unless you repent, you will all likewise perish."

—Luke 13:1-5 (ESV)

As you can see from this passage, Jesus specifically rejects the argument that suffering means God is punishing you for sin. God permits the consequences of human folly (and yes, sin), and this permission includes crime and injustice (verses 1-3). God permits crime—and all other manner of sinful behavior—to occur because he has given us the ability to make choices, even though he knows that we often choose evil over good.

Moreover, God's permissive will, as seen in verses 4 and 5, includes accidents and natural disasters. The earth still groans under the curse from the fall, and earthquakes, fires, floods, and so on are the result of a natural world under sin. Disease, too, is apparently a part of the fall:

✝
📖

God saw how corrupt the earth was, for every creature had corrupted its way on the earth.
—Genesis 6:12 (HCSB)

But God does not necessarily appoint these tragic events. In some cases he might, but it is a mistake to assume automatically that when anything bad happens, God wanted it to or even caused it. "Why did God want this to happen?" is therefore a fallacy, resting on a false assumption. And so, it is doubly wrong to assume that God wanted some personal evil to occur in order to punish someone. We simply cannot know that. We must rest in his love:

✝
📖

In the world you will have tribulation. But take heart; I have overcome the world.
—John 16:33 (ESV)

And lest we forget, the reality is that, as a result of both angelic and human disobedience, evil is working against what God would like to see.

✝
📖

We know that we are of God, and that the whole world lies in the power of the evil one.
—1 John 5:19 (NASB)

Satan is working overtime because he knows his time is limited:

✝
📖

Be of sober spirit, be on the alert. Your adversary, the devil, prowls around like a roaring lion, seeking someone to devour.
—1 Peter 5:8 (NASB)

The pains of life will come to everyone. Sin is real, evil is real, and Satan is real. But those who love God have a helper and a deliverer:

✝
📖

The one who commits sin is of the Devil, for the Devil has sinned from the beginning. The Son of God was revealed for this purpose: to destroy the Devil's works.
—1 John 3:8 (HCSB)

Remember that one of the requests in the Lord's prayer is to "deliver us from the evil one" (Matthew 6:13, HCSB).

It is important to remember, however, that, even though God permits much evil (and much good) to occur in our fallen world, that does not mean that he permits everything. Both good and bad are subject to his will, and he can stop or prevent whatever he wants. The writer of Hebrews says that he needs to help his audience grow in maturity, "and this we will do if God permits" (Hebrews 6:3, HCSB).

God's permissive will comes into play whenever we make plans. A Biblical example occurs when the Apostle Paul tells those at Ephesus that he hopes to see them but can't stay any longer now: "But taking leave of them and saying, 'I will return to you again if God wills,' he set sail from Ephesus" (Acts 18:21, NASB).

God's executive will.

This aspect of God's will covers those events and outcomes that God does indeed appoint or produce by fiat. When he created the universe, for example, it was spoken into existence by executive determination:

✝
📖

And God said, "Let there be light," and there was light.

—Genesis 1:3 (ESV)

Another example would be Jesus' healing by divine will:

✝
📖

When he came down from the mountain, great crowds followed him. And behold, a leper came to him and knelt before him, saying, "Lord, if you will,

you can make me clean." And Jesus stretched out his hand and touched him, saying, "I will; be clean." And immediately his leprosy was cleansed.
—Matthew 8:1-3 (ESV)

Paul refers to the executive aspect of God's will in Romans 9:19b when he quotes a hypothetical critic, "For who can resist his [God's] will?" (HCSB).

God's executive will is so powerful that there is no resisting it. That's why when God announces it, it often includes contingencies or conditions that govern his intentions. The condition often involves his promised response to the choices of his creatures:

†
📖

See, I have set before you today life and good, death and evil. If you obey the commandments of the Lord your God that I command you today . . . then you shall live and multiply, and the Lord your God will bless you. . . . But if your heart turns away . . . you shall surely perish. . . . I have set before you life and death, blessing and curse. Therefore choose life, that you and your offspring may live. . . .
—Deuteronomy 30:15-20 (ESV)

Implications for prayer.

This seemingly off-the-topic excursion from prayer to a look at God's will becomes relevant when we see the several implications for prayer that it entails.

1. Pray to know God's will.

Instead of asking that God will approve our will, we should pray that our lives align with God's preferential will for us. That is, instead of praying, "Lord, may you approve this plan of mine," we should pray, "Lord, let me know your will in this." God has blessings standing by, if we will avail ourselves of them by getting to know them:

†
📖
I know the plans that I have for you, declares the Lord. They are plans for peace and not disaster, plans to give you a future filled with hope. Then you will call to me. You will come and pray to me, and I will hear you. When you look for me, you will find me. When you wholeheartedly seek me, I will let you find me, declares the Lord.
—Jeremiah 29:11-14 (GW)

2. Sin can short circuit God's wishes.

We should not assume that everything that happens is God's best desire for us or for others. He might be disciplining us (Hebrews 12:5-13), but this fallen world filled with the sins of others and ourselves, produces pain and loss that is not God's will. Some people are not saved, but that's not God's will:

†
📖
In the same way, it is not the will of your Father in heaven that one of these little ones perish.
—Matthew 18:14 (HCSB)

3. Evil on earth is most likely God's permissive will.

We should not assume that any disaster or evil is God's preferential or executive will, when it is most likely only his permissive will.

✝
📖
But I say to you, love your enemies and pray for
those who persecute you, so that you may be sons of
your Father who is in heaven; for He causes His sun
to rise on the evil and the good, and sends rain on
the righteous and the unrighteous.
— Matthew 5:44-45 (NASB)

4. We should pray for understanding.

We must pray and study to discern, if possible,
which events in our lives involve which aspects of
God's will, knowing that we cannot always understand. Remember the proverb, "The central work of life
is interpretation."

When understanding is not possible, we must accept both the good and the bad events and ask God to
turn both to his glory and our spiritual improvement.

✝
📖
But resist him [the devil], firm in your faith,
knowing that the same experiences of suffering are
being accomplished by your brethren who are in the
world.
— 1 Peter 5:8-9 (NASB)

5. God knows everything.

Even though God permits many things he does not
appoint, he is still sovereign and in control. He knows
everything that goes on, even when he does not interfere:

†
📖

Aren't two sparrows sold for a penny? Yet not one
of them falls to the ground without your Father's
consent.
                              —Matthew 10:29 (HCSB)

†
📖

Five sparrows are sold for just two pennies, but God
doesn't forget a one of them.
                              —Luke 12:6 (CEV)

And, when asked, he often does interfere, for that is
one of the main purposes of prayer, to ask for and get
God's help.

6. We must remember eternity.

Remember that God's scale and context includes
another, eternal existence for us. Paul says:

We know that God is always at work for the good of
everyone who loves him.
                              —Romans 8:28a (CEV)

However, that is not a guarantee that our difficulties
will be turned to good in this life. God might choose to
bring good from bad only after we have met him in the
Kingdom.

Regardless of which aspect of God's will results in
the challenges or even the disasters we face, we trust
God, for faith means trust, and the negatives of this life
when compared with an eternity of peace can be seen
as mere irritants.

✟✟✟

Chapter 13 Questions for Thought and Discussion
1. Before you read this chapter, how would you have explained God's will?
2. Has the discussion in this chapter changed your view or understanding of God's will? If not, why not? If so, why and how?
3. Suppose you and a friend are discussing a mutual acquaintance who has just been diagnosed with a chronic disease. Your friend asks, "Why does God want this to happen?" How would you reply?

Chapter 13 Activities
1. Ask ten friends how they would define "God's will."
    A. What do they have in common?
    B. How do their understandings differ?
    C. Do any of them reflect a multiple-aspect view?

Chapter 13 Group Activities
1. Discuss how capable group members think they are at discerning God's will for their lives.
2. As a group, locate Scriptures that involve dramatic events (war, new kings, disease, rises to power, etc.) and see if you can agree together about which aspect of God's will was involved in each case.
3. Look up the following verses and for each one discuss as a group whether the verse refers to God's preferential, permissive, or executive will. If some are indeterminate, explain.

Mark 3:35
Romans 1:10
Romans 12:2
Romans 15:32

1 Peter 2:15
1 Peter 4:2
Colossians 4:12
2 Timothy 1:1
Hebrews 10:36
1 Peter 4 :19
1 John 2:17
1 Corinthians 1:1
2 Corinthians 1:1
Ephesians 1:1
Ephesians 6:6
Colossians 1:1
1 Thessalonians 4:3

14

Example Prayers

With a phone in your pocket, you talk to anyone in the world in just a few seconds. With a prayer in your heart, you can talk to God in an instant.
— Anonymous

This chapter contains several examples of prayers for group experience. They are only slightly more formal than personal prayers, but because they are to represent everyone in a group praying in agreement with each other, the language and tone reflect that.

As with all the other prayers in this book, use them as they are, alter them to fit the circumstances, or use them as models or idea sources for writing your own prayers.

Prayers about change.

Change is everywhere, and often the change is not for the better. And even when it is, making the necessary accommodations to it can be challenging and uncomfortable. These prayers seek God's help in facing and negotiating those inevitable changes which arrive constantly.

ಇಂ 🕊 ೞ
A PRAYER ABOUT CHANGE

Lord, you know that change can be unsettling and even fearful for us. Change involves leaving the familiar and entering the unknown. But we rest in the knowledge that every change is known to you and that you hold the future clearly in mind. So we take comfort in trusting you to be present with us through each new event and circumstance, and ask that whatever changes we face, they will all be in your divine and holy will. In Jesus' name. Amen.

ಇಂ 🕊 ೞ
ANOTHER PRAYER ABOUT CHANGE

Lord, we ask for your strength and support as we face the changes of life. We admit that we don't like some of the changes we face. But for every change, and especially the ones that cause us grief or pain or simply inconvenience, we pray that you will be sovereign in and through them, giving us your grace and mercy where we are severely tested. May we accept those changes that are out of our control, and seek your guidance and help to shape the ones we can affect. And may we always remember, whatever we face now, that our final change will be the translation of our bodies and souls into your eternal kingdom. May it come, in Jesus' name. Amen.

ಇಂ 🕊 ೞ
A THIRD PRAYER ABOUT CHANGE

Dear Lord, change is everywhere in our lives. Some of it we welcome and some of it we resist. Many of these changes, even the changes we choose, cause us stress and tension and effort. But, Lord, change one more thing in our lives—change our hearts to trust in you through our lives of change, to understand that you are with us in every circumstance of life. Be our strength and guide us in all the changes we face, and may we see your hand and your goodness behind them all. In Jesus' name. Amen.

 හ 🕊 infty

A FINAL PRAYER ABOUT CHANGE

Our Father, we pray to you today as we face change—and therefore uncertainty—and therefore fear. We pray that you will remind us that you are sovereign over all the earth and all the changes in it. And as we worship you and your will in our lives, help us to remember that because this change that we now face is in your hands, there is no reason for us to fear. Comfort and strengthen us, O Lord, in this knowledge, and continue to exercise your perfect will, in the changes we face and everywhere. In Jesus' name, we thank you. Amen.

Prayers about love.

We often enter into conversations and proceed to use words whose meaning we assume everyone knows. However, many common words, because they are used so often by so many, have different shades of meaning or even different meanings. *Love* is one of those words. These prayers help to clarify and focus the believer's ideas about love.

 හ 🕊 infty

A PRAYER ABOUT LOVE

Dear Lord, you are indeed our loving Father and loving Savior. You define for us the nature, meaning, and actions of love. If only we could imitate you more fully and live out the commands of Jesus to love each other, we could enjoy the true meaning of

Christian love. Help us, Lord, to understand that love does not mean gathering in things or services or even feelings for ourselves. Help us to see that love means giving to other people, treasuring, serving, and valuing them as fellow creatures made in your image. May we share ourselves with those in the faith and those in the world in such a way that they can feel the love of Christ within us. In Jesus' name. Amen.

ജ 🕊 ര
ANOTHER PRAYER ABOUT LOVE

Dear Lord, what word is so abused as the word *love*? The word that was made to refer to the precious bond between husband and wife and parent and child and to our holy connection with you, the God of the universe, is instead employed to mask and even sugarcoat the sinful behaviors that those who indulge them are afraid to describe by their proper names. We ask, O Lord, that you will help us to re-purify the meaning of love by our living out its true significance in our relationships here on earth and with you in heaven. Give us truly loving hearts in the true meaning of love. Help us to know love in the way that you are love. In Jesus' name. Amen.

Prayers about sin.

It is safe to say that, regardless of how long we have been saved, we still sin. Our sanctification is a process that takes time. So, we must often come before the throne of God and seek his forgiveness. These prayers seeking forgiveness are therefore applicable individually and for groups of Christians.

ᔥ 🕊 ᕫ

A PRAYER ABOUT THE FORGIVENESS OF SIN

Dear Lord, you know well that we are all sinners. If we manage to avoid sins of action, we commit heart sins—such as envy, evil thoughts, and pride. Forgive us, we pray, for such lapses, and remake our hearts so that we might eliminate those sinful thoughts and be delivered from the frustration and bitterness they produce in us. Thank you for being a God of love, mercy, and forgiveness. And may we look upon others in the way you look upon us. In Jesus' name. Amen.

ᔥ 🕊 ᕫ

ANOTHER PRAYER ABOUT FORGIVENESS OF SIN

Lord, we ask you today to forgive us for the sin of heartlessness. When we think of those who have sinned against us, we are often hard hearted and slow to forgive. Yet we forgive ourselves quickly enough for the same sins against others. Where you are slow to anger and quick to forgive, we are the opposite. In fact, we often sin in the way we treat those who sin against us. Jesus tells us to forgive if we want to be forgiven, to take the plank out of our own eye, and to forgive a repentant offender seven times a day. Truly, we worship a God of patience, compassion, and understanding. Help us to be as forgiving, with our whole hearts, as our mighty God and Savior is, and not to repay a sin with a sin. Thank you, Lord. In Jesus' name we pray. Amen.

ᔥ 🕊 ᕫ

A THIRD PRAYER ABOUT FORGIVENESS OF SIN

Our precious Father in heaven, we come to you once more in the full embarrassment of sin. We have transgressed and disappointed you yet once again, perhaps with the very sins we were criticizing our neighbor for. Lord, forgiveness is the first thing we ask for. Another thing is that you will turn us away from the path of disobedience and place our feet firmly on the road to righteousness. Send the power of your Holy Spirit to inspire us to goodness and to keep from those sins we find so attractive. We thank you for being a God of mercy to forgive us in our weakness, a God of truth to instruct us on the right path, and a God of power to keep us safe from the evil one. In Jesus' name. Amen.

Prayers about forgiveness.

As the prayers above reveal, praying for forgiveness is a common event, both as individuals and in groups. But in addition to praying that our own sins will be forgiven, we can also pray that we will forgive those who wrong us. A formal prayer like this in a group setting can bring repentance and healing among those who participate as they forgive each other.

ဆ ⅄ ભ
A PRAYER FOR FORGIVING OTHERS

Dear Lord, in the prayer you taught your first disciples, you included "forgive us our debts as we forgive our debtors," showing the importance of forgiveness and the linkage between your forgiving us and our forgiving others. Help us, then, to be forgiving, not to hold a grudge or to withhold forgiveness, even to those who might not even acknowledge that they have wronged us. May we imitate you in mercy and grace, and not only forgive but pray for those who cause us harm. In the name of that great Righteous One, Jesus Christ, who sacrificed his very life in order to forgive us and account us righteous. Amen.

Here is another prayer seeking God's help in overcoming our unwillingness to forgive others.

☙ 🕊 ❧
A PRAYER SEEKING HELP TO FORGIVE

Lord God, sometimes we find it difficult to forgive others who have harmed us. Our resentment, righteous anger, feeling of betrayal, and plain old pride, all join together against the idea of forgiving the hurt. But we know from your word that you have commanded us to forgive those who injure us. And, we know from experience that this command is for our own good because we cannot have peace of heart until we forgive others. Deliver us from the grudges and resentments of unforgiveness, those feelings of ill will that eat at our hearts. And thank you for being our model of mercy by sending your son Jesus to save us, making friends instead of enemies of us, loving us instead of resenting us, and forgiving us instead of condemning us. In his name we pray. Amen.

Of course, we all need forgiveness for our own sins. But as the prayer below shows, the need for forgiveness is complex and consists of multiple sinners and multiple forgivers. These include the need for:

- God to forgive us of intentional sins
- God to forgive us of unintentional sins
- God's help in our forgiving others who have wronged us
- God's forgiveness of those who have wronged us

- God's help in forgiving ourselves

A Prayer For Forgiving Us and Others

Dear Lord, you know we are weak and no matter how hard we try, we still fall into sin and need your forgiveness anew. So we ask you yet again to forgive us of our sins, those committed deliberately and those carelessly, and that you will forgive those who have wronged us. And, knowing that you have forgiven us and those who have wronged us, help us to forgive them also, and be free of guilt, and shame, and grudging, and resentment. Finally, teach us to forgive ourselves and to find peace in you. In Jesus' name. Amen.

Prayers about trust.

It is sometimes said that trust is the most important, though less acknowledged, virtue. While the three traditional Christian virtues are faith, hope, and love (see 1 Corinthians 13:13), trust is the foundation of all three. Faith *is* trust, hope is built on trust, and love embodies trust. Without trust, in other words, there can be no faith, no hope, and no love.

These prayers are especially pertinent when a believer suffers the pains and sorrows of life, through illness, loss, or other disaster.

A Prayer About Trust

Lord, thank you for the people in our lives whom we can trust, because that trust gives us confidence and security in them, and enduring friendship as a result. Bless all the trustworthy people of this world, and help us to live so that we may be counted among them. And thank you most of all, dear Lord, for yourself and for your word, the source and revelation of all that is good and trustworthy. May we always trust in you, with the confidence and assurance you deserve. In Jesus' name. Amen.

ℰ 🕊 ℛ
ANOTHER PRAYER ABOUT TRUST

Lord, help us always to place our trust where we should. Not in riches or possessions, but in fellow believers and in others who are trustworthy. Send us the right people we can place our confidence in. And when our trust turns out to be misplaced, keep us from growing bitter or cynical. Help us instead to turn to those who are worthy of our trust. In all this and in all our lives and activities, dear Lord, help us foremost to trust in you, always assured that you are the one we can trust without worry, concern, or doubt. We know that we cannot always understand your ways, but we know, too, that we can always trust you. That is our faith. In Jesus' name. Amen.

✠✠✠

Chapter 14 Questions for Thought and Discussion

1. Each category of prayer above contains more than one prayer on that theme. For each category, choose one prayer over the others. Explain the basis for your choice (applicability to yourself or your group, emotional resonance, what was included, and so forth).
2. Define faith, hope, love, and trust.
3. Draw a diagram showing the relationship between faith, hope, love, and trust.

4. If you were required to present a discussion about the relationship between faith, hope, love, and trust, how would you describe the relationships between them?

5. Define forgiveness and explain who needs it. Should we "forgive and forget"? Why or why not?

6. Define love. If needed, identify different kinds of love. The table offers some types.

I Love . . .

| my dog | ice cream | good books | my spouse |
| dip chips | my car | good jokes | action flix |

Finally, explain what all these things have in common that causes us to use the word *love* for each one.

Chapter 14 Activity

1. Choose an example prayer from this chapter and analyze it for effectiveness. Sentence by sentence, what works and what doesn't? Explain why in each case.

Chapter 14 Group Activities

1. Choose a prayer from this chapter and analyze it for effectiveness.
    A. What are its strengths?
    B. What are its weaknesses?
    C. How could it be improved?

2. Choose a prayer from this chapter and work as a group to improve it for overall effectiveness.
    A. Can it be made clearer?
    B. Could the focus, the main point, be made clearer?
    C. Could sentences be improved?

15

The Lord's Prayer as a Model

Jesus reminds us that prayer is a little like children coming to their parents.
— *Richard Foster*

When his disciples asked him how to pray, Jesus offered what is now known as the Lord's Prayer as a model. (It should be called the Disciples' Prayer since it was given to them to pray. Jesus did not pray it.)

Here is the prayer in the New American Standard translation (Matthew 6:9-13), together with some commentary.

Our Father who is in heaven

We acknowledge God as our heavenly Father, author of our being, guide and helper and chastiser. As our Father, he loves us as his children. We are family. As a Father, he guides, educates, and disciplines us, and he sees what we need to live and prosper. He listens to our requests when we pray.

Because he is in heaven, we understand that he and his ways are higher than ours. He can see all of history, past, present, and future, at once. So he knows what is good for us and what is not. When we need to make a choice during our journey of life, we can barely see the next step through the darkness. But God can see the entire staircase and where it leads — including the unintended consequences that our choice might involve.

Hallowed be Your name.

This is the first petition or request, that God's name will be kept holy. By asking this, we affirm that we want God to be respected and adored and exalted. We believe that he is all good, all light, with no darkness at all. We take joy in knowing that light floods into darkness, but darkness can never flood into light.

Your kingdom come.

The second petition asks that God's kingdom will be made sovereign on earth. We affirm that he is the proper ruler of heaven and earth, whose kingdom we pray will soon expand to the earth.

Your will be done, On earth as it is in heaven.

The third petition asks that God's will, in all its aspects, will be established on earth, crushing the evil in competition with it, just as his will is done in heaven. This petition also shows our submission to God's will in the request that his will (rather than ours) should be accomplished. And the final clause affirms that God is the ruler of heaven.

Give us this day our daily bread.

The fourth petition represents a change from previous ones, that God be honored in various ways, to personal requests. In this first personal request, Jesus employs figurative language, using bread to stand for food. This usage is a type of metaphor called synecdoche, where a part stands for a whole (bread is part of food). Therefore, the request is for all of our daily food needs. (See page 237 for more on synecdoche.)

But there's more to this request. Jesus uses figurative language intentionally. Consider these Scriptures:

✝
📖

He humbled you and let you be hungry, and fed you with manna which you did not know, nor did your fathers know, that He might make you understand that man does not live by bread alone, but man lives by everything that proceeds out of the mouth of the LORD.
— Deuteronomy 8:3 (NASB)

This tells us that, in addition to physical food, we need spiritual food, coming from God.

✝
📖

But He answered and said, "It is written, 'man shall not live on bread alone, but on every word that proceeds out of the mouth of God.'"
— Matthew 4:4 (NASB)

By quoting Deuteronomy, Jesus reaffirms this truth and points out our need for the spiritual bread of life. This "bread of God" gives us life.

✝
📖

For the bread of God is that which comes down out of heaven, and gives life to the world.
— John 16:33 (NASB)

And what is this "bread of God" this bread that gives life to the world, this bread of life?

†
📖

I am the bread of life.

—John 6:48 (NASB)

The "daily bread," therefore, is not only our daily literal food, but our daily spiritual food, supplied by Jesus, the "bread of life."

†
📖

It is the Spirit who gives life; the flesh profits nothing; the words that I have spoken to you are spirit and are life.

—John 6:63 (NASB)

In this prayer, then, Jesus taught us to ask for daily spiritual food as well as physical food, that we might grow in him every day.

And forgive us our debts, as we also have forgiven our debtors.

What is as important as the food that sustains us, in both the physical and the spiritual sense? The fifth petition seems to answer, forgiveness. Forgive us for our debts, or as some translations render it, our sins. Jesus knows that we are his forgiven sinners who sometimes slip back into sins, so just as we must ask for daily bread, so we must ask for (daily?) forgiveness.

Note also the conditional, "as we also have forgiven our debtors." When we pray the Lord's prayer, we are saying, "Forgive us for our sins against you and others to the same extent that we forgive others who have sinned against us." Ouch.

Of all the petitions and praises in the Lord's prayer, this is the only one that Jesus comments on. And his commentary is about our need to forgive others if we hope to be forgiven by God.

And do not lead us into temptation.

The sixth petition asks God to keep temptation away from us, knowing how weak we are. If temptation does come, we are asking for strength to resist it. The literal meaning seems to be, "Don't let us enter a time of trial."

But deliver us from evil.

The seventh and final petition asks that God will use his power to keep us safe from Satan and the evils of the world. Here we are reminded that God is the author of good, and Satan is the author of evil.

For Yours is the kingdom and the power and the glory forever. Amen.

The concluding sentence of the prayer affirms the rule, dominion, and gloriousness of God.

✠✠✠

Chapter 15 Questions for Thought and Discussion

1. Why do you think Jesus taught the disciples such a short prayer?

2. How comprehensive is the Lord's prayer? Does it omit something that you include in your own prayers?

3. If a stranger asked you, "What is the Lord's prayer about?" how would you summarize it in one sentence?

Chapter 15 Activities

1. Ask ten people to explain the petition, "And forgive us our debts, as we also have forgiven our debtors."

   A. How do they understand the meaning of "debtors"?

   B. What is the response of those who do not understand that Jesus means sins when he says debts? (If necessary, explain that some translations have, "And forgive us our sins, as we have forgiven those who sin against us."

2. Paraphrase (change into your own words) the Lord's prayer. Show it to some others and see what they think.

Chapter 15 Group Activities

1. Discuss with the group what is encompassed by "Your will be done on earth." Does it or does it not include nearly everything we ask God for?

2. Discuss with the group why you think Jesus used *debts* instead of *sins*. As with the term bread, is there more than one kind of debt meant here?

16

Using Imagery and Figurative Language

All these things Jesus spoke to the crowds in parables, and He did not speak to them without a parable.
— Matthew 13:34 (NASB)

Those who write and deliver public prayers — pastors, missionaries, Christian camp leaders, those who open various meetings — sometimes want to add imagery and figurative language to their prayers in order to make them more memorable. If those present during the prayer (and therefore those who also share in the prayer) are encouraged by the language and imagery to pay close attention, then the prayer can be more impactful. Such prayers can be remembered more easily, and they can have more emotional impact.

As the epigraph above tells us, Jesus used parables extensively in his teaching, and while they confused many of his hearers at the time, we treasure them for their power and memorability, their vividness and ultimately, their clarity.

Imagery.

Imagery is the use of concrete, visual language, language that creates pictures. Using image-invoking words is especially helpful or even necessary in religious discussion and prayers because theology is abstract and abstractions are not visualizable. Compare the following two prayers.

ഇ 🕊 ☙

A PRAYER WITHOUT IMAGERY

Dear Great Being who realized the cosmos, we thank you for our justification through your only progeny and pray that you will advance to completion the sanctification of our spirits. . . .

ഇ 🕊 ☙

A PRAYER WITH IMAGERY

Dear Father, creator of the mountains and valleys, of every flower that blooms and everything else, thank you for our savior Jesus, whose death on the cross paid for all our sins and put us on the road to holiness. Help us to travel that road to its ultimate completion. . . .

Often, images are used as part of figurative language (see the section below), but they can be used just to provide vividness to the ideas being prayed about. For example:

ഇ 🕊 ☙

ANOTHER PRAYER WITH IMAGERY

Dear Heavenly Father, Paul tells us in Romans 1 that your divine qualities can be seen through what you have made. Whether we look up at the stars or down on the earth at the trees and mountains you have created to decorate the earth, we can indeed see your character. The flowered meadows, the scented forests, and the perpetual pounding of the ocean waves against the sandy shore—all these tell of your intelligence, creativity, constancy, and love. We thank you, Lord, for creating such a beautiful world and for giving us the necessary sense of beauty to see it. All glory and honor be yours now and forever. In Jesus' name. Amen.

Figurative language.

Figurative language includes the use of various rhetorical devices that reach beyond the literal and make comparisons between spiritual ideas (which are abstract) and specific images (which are concrete). The advantage is that, while abstract ideas do not produce images in our minds, concrete images do. When something abstract is mentioned—strength, money, food—no image is produced in our minds. But when something concrete is mentioned—a hammer, a pearl, a loaf of bread—we see an image in our minds. Image-creating words are easier to understand and remember than abstract words. Figurative language, then, makes the discussion of abstract ideas easier to comprehend.

The recommendation to use figurative language needs no more support than God's word in Scripture, because the Bible is filled with figures of speech. So let's turn our attention to how the most common devices work.

Simile.

A simile briefly compares something unfamiliar with something familiar in order to clarify the unfamiliar thing. Similes are invoked by using a word of comparison, most often *like* or *as*. And, as with other types of figurative language, simile often uses something visual and concrete to clarify something less visual or even abstract.

In the quotation below from Psalm 68, notice how visual the image of wax melting in front of a fire is compared with the plain "let the wicked perish":

†
📖

As smoke is driven away, so drive them away; As wax melts before the fire, So let the wicked perish before God.
— Psalm 68:2 (NASB)

The image of wax melting can be visualized and therefore remembered, making remembrance of the wicked perishing easier also.

In the following quotation, "each of us has turned to his own way" doesn't create a picture in our minds; but the image of sheep having "gone astray" does produce a mental picture:

†
📖

All of us like sheep have gone astray,
Each of us has turned to his own way;
— Isaiah 53:6a (NASB)

Here, we see the image of a bunch of sheep wandering off in every direction, making the idea of our going spiritually astray much more vivid and impactful.

Sometimes a simile uses *than* to make the comparison:

†
📖

Men of low degree are only vanity and men of rank are a lie; In the balances they go up; They are together lighter than breath.

—Psalm 62:9 (NASB)

"Lighter than breath" strikes a memorable comparison.

ঙ 🕊 ন
A PRAYER BEFORE READING A SCRIPTURE PASSAGE

We thank and praise you, Lord, for your word in the Bible, for it is more than an encouragement; it is like a flowing stream of cool water in the desert, inviting us to drink as much as we want. It satisfies our souls while imparting your truth. Bless our understanding as your word is read. In Jesus' name. Amen.

Analogy.

An analogy might be thought of as an extended simile, where several points of similarity are identified between the familiar and the unfamiliar idea, with the express purpose of clarifying the unfamiliar more completely than a simile usually does.

In the following example, Jesus compares the sceptics of the current generation to willful children:

†
📖

But to what shall I compare this generation? It is like children sitting in the market places, who call out to the other children, and say, "We played the flute for you, and you did not dance; we sang a dirge, and you did not mourn." For John came neither eating

nor drinking, and they say, "He has a demon!" The Son of Man came eating and drinking, and they say, "Behold, a gluttonous man and a drunkard, a friend of tax collectors and sinners!" Yet wisdom is vindicated by her deeds.
—Matthew 11:16-19 (NASB)

Jesus' parables are often analogies, which he uses in part because theological concepts are by nature abstract and difficult to grasp. Matthew Chapter 13 records many of Jesus' parables, together with explanations of a number of them. Here is one of the shorter ones:

✝
📖

Again, the kingdom of heaven is like a dragnet cast into the sea, and gathering fish of every kind; and when it was filled, they drew it up on the beach; and they sat down and gathered the good fish into containers, but the bad they threw away. So it will be at the end of the age; the angels will come forth and take out the wicked from among the righteous, and will throw them into the furnace of fire; in that place there will be weeping and gnashing of teeth.
—Matthew 13:47-50 (NASB)

ඞ 🕊 ඥ
A PRAYER FOR GUIDANCE

Dear Lord, we come to you today seeking your guidance. We find ourselves like children lost in the forest as darkness approaches. We are wandering in different directions, not knowing the path that will lead us to deliverance. We humbly ask therefore, that you will put your Spirit of wisdom and knowledge on us and lead us to a successful decision. We thank you and praise you in Jesus' name. Amen.

Metaphor.

Metaphor is an especially dramatic figure of speech because, unlike a simile which says one thing is *like* another, a metaphor says one thing *is* another, equating them imaginatively.

Note in the passage below that Jesus does not say the disciples are "*like* the salt of the earth," but that they "*are* the salt of the earth."

✝
📖

You are the salt of the earth; but if the salt has become tasteless, how can it be made salty again? It is no longer good for anything, except to be thrown out and trampled under foot by men.
—Matthew 5:13 (NASB)

Again, note in the following example that the metaphor says that the false prophets *are* wolves, not simply *like* wolves. The equating of the two is quite dramatic.

✝
📖

Beware of the false prophets, who come to you in sheep's clothing, but inwardly are ravenous wolves. You will know them by their fruits.
—Matthew 7:15-16a (NASB)

Sometimes the metaphorical equation of two things is implied rather than put in the form of X is Y. For example, the last part of the quotation above contains an implied metaphor, where *fruits* stands for *deeds*. The implied equating is "their deeds are fruits." Another example of an implied metaphor comes from Psalm 17:

✝

📖

Keep me as the apple of the eye; Hide me in the shadow of Your wings.
—Psalm 17:8 (NASB)

In this metaphor, God is imaginatively compared to a bird that nestles its young under its wings. An explicit metaphor here would be unseemly: "God is a bird under whose wings I hide."

And Jesus metaphorically identifies himself as a beast of burden, wearing a double yoke to pull the plow along with another beast:

✝

📖

Come to Me, all who are weary and heavy-laden, and I will give you rest. Take My yoke upon you and learn from Me, for I am gentle and humble in heart, and you will find rest for your souls. For My yoke is easy and My burden is light.
—Matthew 11:28-30 (NASB)

Here is another implied metaphor, where leaven (which spreads through the entire loaf of dough) is equated with the false teaching of the Pharisees, which can spread and corrupt everyone:

✝

📖

And He was giving orders to them, saying, "Watch out! Beware of the leaven of the Pharisees and the leaven of Herod."
—Mark 8:15 (NASB)

Note, too, that figures can be mixed together, as in this passage from the Psalms:

†

📖

His speech was smoother than butter, But his heart was war; His words were softer than oil, Yet they were drawn swords.

—Psalm 55:21 (NASB)

This passage mixes similes (where the subjects are connected to the images by *than*) and metaphors. "His words were like drawn swords" would have been much less dramatic than saying "they *were* drawn swords."

ଋଡ଼ ଈ

A PRAYER FOR SPIRITUAL COURAGE

Dear Lord, sometimes the world seems to be against me, attacking my faith and your truth. Help me, O God, not to shrink away or to hide my head in silence, but to be your warrior, engaging the army of lies confidently with the sword of your word and the shield of faith. May I grow each day in spiritual power, fighting ever more effectively, until our enemies are convinced of your truth, turn their hearts around, and join us in the fight. In the name of Jesus my savior I pray. Amen.

Metonymy.

Metonymy (meh TAWN uh mee) is a type of metaphor which describes one thing by naming something associated with the thing rather than naming the thing itself.

✝
📖

By the sweat of your face You will eat bread. . . .
　　　　　　　　　　　　　　—Genesis 3:19a (NASB)

Here, *the sweat of your face* is a metonymy which substitutes sweat to mean *hard labor* because sweat is associated with hard labor.

In the following two examples, *walk* is a metonymy for *live*, since walking is associated with living.

✝
📖

He who trusts in his own heart is a fool,
But he who walks wisely will be delivered.
　　　　　　　　　　　　　　—Proverbs 28:26 (NASB)

✝
📖

The Pharisees and the scribes asked Him, "Why do Your disciples not walk according to the tradition of the elders, but eat their bread with impure hands?"
　　　　　　　　　　　　　　—Mark 7:5 (NASB)

In the passage below, *blood* is a metonymy for *life*, since the life of a person is closely associated with the blood.

✝
📖

When Pilate saw that he was accomplishing nothing, but rather that a riot was starting, he took water and washed his hands in front of the crowd, saying, "I am innocent of this Man's blood; see to that yourselves."
　　　　　　　　　　　　　　—Matthew 27:24 (NASB)

The following example prayer lays on the metonymies a little too thick, but it does allow you to get a sense of the figure.

ఴ 🕊 ಞ

A PRAYER WITH METONYMY

Dear God, we are so thankful that we can connect to heaven's cell tower anytime we want, day or night and that you are there to pick up the phone personally. We rejoice in knowing that we can come to the throne as often as we need to—which for most of us occurs at every tick mark on the face of the clock. Direct us, O Lord. Show us the true North on the compass, and move our journey along by it. Thank you again in the name of Jesus. Amen.

Synecdoche.

Synecdoche (sin EK doe key) is a type of metaphor that substitutes a part of something for the whole, the whole for a part, or the material for the thing made. For example, in the sentence below, *ox* and *donkey* are synecdoches for all livestock, such as sheep, goats, and other domestic animals:

✝
📖

If you meet your enemy's ox or his donkey wandering away, you shall surely return it to him.
—Exodus 23:4 (NASB)

And in the Lord's prayer, *bread* refers not simply to bread, but to food (part-for-whole substitution), and even more, to all our needs, bread being the crucial symbol of our needs (as opposed to merely our wants).

†
📖

Give us this day our daily bread.
— Matthew 6:11 (NASB)

Occasionally, metonymy overlaps with hyperbole (ex-aggeration), as when the whole is stated in place of a part. In this example below, *the world* is used in place of *many people*, at least partly because to the Pharisees it must have felt like everyone had begun to follow Jesus:

†
📖

So the Pharisees said to one another, "You see that you are not doing any good; look, the world has gone after Him."
— John 12:19 (NASB)

Finally, some rhetoricians do not distinguish between metonymy and synecdoche because there can be unclear cases. For example, in the following passage, is *tongue* a part-for-whole synecdoche (tongue is a part of speaking) or one thing associated with another thing (tongue associated with speech)?

†
📖

And my tongue shall declare Your righteousness
And Your praise all day long.
— Psalm 35:28 (NASB)

The point is to create effective, visual, interesting pray-ers that resonate with your audience — memorable im-ages that speak to the imagination, the emotions, and the mind. Images that draw you or others closer to God are good images, regardless of their technical classification.

ళు 🕊 ଓଃ

A PRAYER WITH SYNECDOCHE

Our father God, we are grateful to you for giving us eyes into the faith, that we might see and understand your truth that puts the key into the lock of our spiritual imprisonment and that sets us free. The locks have popped open and our chains have fallen off. Help us never again to desire the new, polished, shiny, and so popular chains being offered to every credulous sinner. May we always keep the pages of your word close by. In Jesus' name. Amen.

Personification.

Personification is another type of metaphor, in which something non-human (idea, object, animal, God) is identified with a human characteristic in order to clarify the non-human thing.

In the following Scripture, wisdom, which is an abstract concept that produces no images in our minds when we read the word, is personified by discussing it as if it were a human being, a woman, addressing the people in the street:

†
📖

Wisdom calls out in the street; she raises her voice in the public squares. She cries out above the commotion; she speaks at the entrance of the city gates: "How long, foolish ones, will you love ignorance? How long will you mockers enjoy mocking and you fools hate knowledge?

— Proverbs 1:20-22 (HCSB)

Notice how much livelier and more vivid this is than saying something like, "How long will foolish people mock wisdom?"

In this next example, note the joy expressed by personified nature:

✝

📖

For you will go out with joy And be led forth with peace; The mountains and the hills will break forth into shouts of joy before you, And all the trees of the field will clap their hands.

—Isaiah 55:12 (NASB)

The image of trees clapping their hands is difficult to see in the mind's eye, but we do see trees, at least, and perhaps hand clapping.

✝

📖

Now we know that whatever the Law says, it speaks to those who are under the Law, so that every mouth may be closed and all the world may become accountable to God.

—Romans 3:19 (NASB)

Next, note that God himself can be personified, in this case by implying a physical body through the mention of an arm. How else can we see in our minds a picture of a spiritual being?

✝

📖

Ah Lord GOD! Behold, You have made the heavens and the earth by Your great power and by Your outstretched arm! Nothing is too difficult for You.

—Jeremiah 32:17 (NASB)

And here is an implied personification of God, where Jesus imaginatively says that God has a body that sits on a throne:

✝
📖

And whoever swears by heaven, swears both by the throne of God and by Him who sits upon it.
— Matthew 23:22 (NASB)

One thing to note about the use of figurative language in cases like this is that it allows us to have some concept, at least, for thinking about God and the theological abstractions that belong to him.

ಸಂ 🕊 ೞ
A PRAYER WITH PERSONIFICATION

Our heavenly Father, thank you so much for keeping a watchful eye on me and my family. How many traps have you pointed out to us when we were close to falling in. When we sought your will through reading Scripture and praying, you have more than once reached out and pulled us back from a disaster. So we come to you once again, asking for your guidance in this decision. Look down the roads we must choose from and let us know the one that keeps us in your will. Again, we thank you with deepest gratitude and warmest love. In Jesus' name. Amen.

Suggestions for using figurative language in prayers.

The English poet, George Herbert, was also a preacher; he wrote *The Country Parson*, a manual of instruction for new ministers. In his discussion of teaching by analogy, he underscores the importance not only of using such images, but the necessity of making them clear to the audience. He says:

> The Country Parson is full of all knowledge. They say, it is an ill mason that refuseth any stone: And there is no knowledge, but, in a skillful hand, serves either positively as it is, or else to illustrate some other knowledge. He condescends even to the knowledge of tillage and pastorage, and makes great use of them in teaching, because people by what they understand are best led to what they understand not.[5]

The best figures of speech use common and familiar images, simple and focused comparisons, vivid, picture-creating words, and fresh and, if possible, new images.

Common. As we have seen, analogies especially, but all other figures too, should connect the concept you want to clarify (or otherwise compare) to an image that the audience finds accessible. The first suggestion for using figurative language in prayers, then, is to find images that the audience of the prayer can understand. This means images that are common to the audience of the prayer, but not clichés or worn out images.

Note in the example below, the imagery would be perfectly understandable to a jet engine mechanic, but possibly not to a psychology professor or a pastry baker.

---

[5] George Herbert, *A Priest to the Temple* (1652); rpt. in *The Works of George Herbert*, ed. F. E. Hutchinson, Oxford: Clarendon Press, 1941, Chapter 4, p. 228 (spelling modernized).

ଽୖ ゾ ୬
A PRAYER WITH UNCOMMON IMAGERY

Oh Lord, the criticism we receive, like the bypass air on a high-bypass turbofan engine, sometimes spares us the heat and stress of the high-pressure compressor, only to be mixed with the gasses of gossip blasting out of the exhaust nozzle. . . .

Compare the above prayer snippet to the one below, exploring the same theme:

ଽୖ ゾ ୬
A PRAYER WITH ACCESSIBLE IMAGERY

Oh Lord, sometimes our critics seem to plant the prickly thorn bushes just far enough apart to let us get by with only a few scratches, only to discover as we jump through that we have leaped into their burning pit. . . .

Simple. Imagery should be just that, words that create easily formed images in the audience's mind. Don't overelaborate the image for no reason. Note how the following example gets caught up in its own imagery, ultimately confusing the point of the prayer:

ଽୖ ゾ ୬
A PRAYER WITH A COMPLEX IMAGE

Oh Lord, we live by the click of the escapement in our watches, powered by the tense, spiraled mainspring that pushes the gears to spin, ultimately moving the hands on the face of the watch, saying, "Your time is leaving you!"

Contrast the above with this:

ɞ 🕊 ଓ

A PRAYER WITH A NICE AND SIMPLE IMAGE

O Lord, why does my time continue to strut in a fixed step even though it's leaving me behind? . . .

Vivid. To be vivid, the imagery should usually be more specific than general. To enable the participant in your prayer to see bright and clear images, make them dazzle.

ɞ 🕊 ଓ

A PRAYER THAT IS LESS VIVID

Our little Sally was like a flower that bloomed with promise, but was picked before her time. . . .

ɞ 🕊 ଓ

A VIVID PRAYER

Our little Sally was like a golden-yellow tulip showing her smiling sunny petals to all who saw her. But she was called away to glow in a heavenly bouquet, too valuable to be left here on earth any longer. . . .

Fresh. This is the most difficult characteristic. So many metaphors have been used and overused that it's a challenge to create images that are both effective and novel. However, even basic figures can become new by the way they are employed. Consider the difference:

ɞ 🕊 ଓ

A PRAYER WITH A COMMON IMAGE

Lord, life is a journey, and we need to travel through it with your help. . . .

ℬ 🕊 ℭ
A PRAYER WITH FRESHER IMAGERY

Dear God, we realize that we have a choice of roads to travel. There's the eight-lane, well-traveled constantly repaved super highway that rolls along smoothly, and there's the rocky, sometimes muddy path up a too-steep hill, not well taken care of. Those who choose the steep path breathe heavily with the difficulty of the labor. But they climb with an unspeakable joy because they know they will eventually reach the Kingdom of Heaven. Those who cruise down the super highway have an easy trip, but they are empty and unhappy, and their destination is hell. . . .

You'll recognize the imagery above adapted from Jesus' imagery in Matthew Chapter 7:

✝
📖

Enter through the narrow gate; for the gate is wide and the way is broad that leads to destruction, and there are many who enter through it. For the gate is small and the way is narrow that leads to life, and there are few who find it.

—Matthew 7:13-14 (NASB)

The point is, you can use common metaphors and still be fresh.

Figurative language should not be used just to show off or sound impressive. A goal like that is almost guaranteed to result in a negative effect. The purpose of figurative language is to improve the clarity of the point you are making and to make it more memorable through imagery. Clarity and memorability promote effective communication.

✜✜✜

Chapter 16 Questions for Thought and Discussion

1. What is your response to someone who says that adding imagery to prayers makes them "insincere"?
2. Have you been encouraged by this chapter to add some vivid metaphors or analogies to your public prayers? Why or why not?
3. Besides allowing the hearers of the prayer to see images in their minds, what effects do images have on those who hear the prayers?

Chapter 16 Activities

1. Using the images below, create some useful and fresh metaphors that clarify spiritual or Biblical principles:
   • journey
   • rock
   • battle
   • writing
   • time
2. Locate six examples of figurative language in the Bible (Old and New Testaments). Rewrite each one, eliminating the figure and substituting it with the literal meaning, as discovered by the context.
Example:

✝

Then Jesus again spoke to them, saying, "I am the Light of the world; he who follows Me will not walk in the darkness, but will have the Light of life."
—John 8:12 (NASB)

Rewrite:

> I have the knowledge that will bring eternal life to those who believe. Those who follow me will not live in ignorance, but will know the truth about God and salvation.

Now explain the difference between the two versions.

Chapter 16 Group Activities

1. As a group, look through the four Gospels and locate as many similes, analogies, metaphors, metonymies, synecdoches, and personifications as you can in ten minutes.

2. Discuss the figures you found in the activity above. How effective is each one? What about the effective figures makes them work so well?

Write your own prayers here.

_____

_____

_____

_____

_____

_____

_____

_____

_____

_____

_____

_____

_____

_____

_____

_____

17

A Sample Prayer Journal

Pale ink is better than the most retentive memory.
— Confucius

Below are two sample pages from a two-page-per-day prayer journal that will allow you to keep track of your prayers and grow spiritually each day. Feel free to make photo copies of these pages and create your own journal.

Here is a description of the various divisions in the journal.

Today's Thought.

Use this space to enter a proverb (Biblical or otherwise), an idea, a word of exhortation or encouragement, or a personal spiritual goal. Examples:

- Strive to be excellent.
- Be a light to everyone today.
- Resist the devil and he will flee from you.
- What you do is more important than what you say.

Praises and Thanksgivings.

Use this section to praise God for his many blessings, to be thankful for all you have, and to rejoice in

God's love and mercy. Ideas include food, housing, freedom, friends, knowledge, salvation, healing. . . .

Scriptures.

If you are moved by two or three verses in your daily Bible reading, you can write them here, if your writing is sufficiently small. Otherwise you'll have to write down only the verse references.

In this area, record relevant Scriptures related to prayer requests, verses that stand out from your Bible reading, verses that the Holy Spirit has brought to your mind today, or verses that are especially important to you today.

Prayers for Myself.

Write your personal requests in this section. Remember that God welcomes both large and small requests, so if you're starting a new job today (or just got fired), ask the Lord for help. And, if you're just feeling a little under the weather, ask the Lord for help.

Lord's Prayer.

Jesus taught his disciples to pray in Matthew 6, where he offers a model prayer that includes several elements. The check boxes cover each of the items Jesus taught us to include when we pray. This section encourages you to cover each of the items at some point during the day, and then confirming their accomplishment with a check mark.

Note that the one item Jesus emphasizes by commenting on it is forgiving those who have sinned against us. This is also the item that we too often neglect to include in our daily prayer life.

New Prayer Requests.

Record new requests for the needs of others, together with people and situations that you have learned are in need of prayer.

Some requests will be "time bound" and expire in the near future ("Please help Jane to have a safe and successful surgery on Wednesday"; "May Tom score well on his exam next week"), while others will be longer term ("Please help Dan and Paula to resolve their differences"; "Please make Sheila's chemotherapy successful").

This section can also be used for a general prayer that will cover the day. It could be for guidance, protection, and health for your loved ones. Or it could be for wisdom for world leaders, the working out of an international situation (poverty, war, disease): Whatever is of most concern to you today.

Ongoing Prayer Requests.

Copy the New Prayer Requests from previous days that are long term or that have not expired. Copying ongoing requests each day allows you to pay attention to them, pray for them as you copy, and refresh the need in your mind.

What I have learned / How I have grown today.

This section encourages you to look back at the end of each day and think about what happened and what you learned from the people and events of the day. How have you grown in maturity, wisdom, knowledge, spiritual understanding? Can you convert what you learned into a proverb or wise summary?

Prayer Journal   Date

Today's Thought

Praises and Thanksgivings

Scriptures

Prayers for Myself

Lord's Prayer: Today I have
- [ ] praised and worshipped God
- [ ] prayed that God's will is done
- [ ] asked for daily needs
- [ ] sought forgiveness for sins
- [ ] forgiven those who wronged me
- [ ] prayed to avoid temptation
- [ ] sought deliverance from evil

New Prayer Requests

Ongoing Prayer Requests

What I have learned / How I have grown today

About the Author

Robert A. Harris taught at the college and university level for more than 25 years. He also worked in the corporate world as an instructional designer, and has consulted as an information architect. He has written several books, including *Marriage in a Nutshell, Glimmerings I,* and *Glimmerings II.* He lives in California with his wife, Marie.

This book is available from Amazon.com and other fine retailers.

Don't worry about anything, but pray about everything. With thankful hearts offer up your prayers and requests to God.

—Philippians 4:6 (NLT)

Colophon
Body Copy Set In
Book Antiqua 11 point
Scriptures, Prayers, and Vignettes Set In
Book Antiqua 10 point
Heads Set In
Franklin Gothic 11 and 12 point bold

www.ingramcontent.com/pod-product-compliance
Lightning Source LLC
Chambersburg PA
CBHW060010050426
42448CB00012B/2690